the new
creation

"THEREFORE IF ANY MAN
IS IN CHRIST,
HE IS A NEW
CREATURE;
THE OLD THINGS
PASSED AWAY;
BEHOLD, NEW THINGS
HAVE COME."
II CORINTHIANS 5:17

Jay Wilson, Evangelist
1233 N. 8th
Bozeman, MT 59715
Ph: 406-581-2930, 406-586-8061,
www.newcreationstudies.org
www.christschurchonline.com
email: jaywilsonbooks@gmail.com

Dear Reader:

This Bible study is the fourth in a series designed to teach you the basics of the New Testament. Because of the importance of this study, and the explosive Biblical concept which it sets forth, it is our fervent prayer that it will accomplish its purpose

The basic conclusions reached in this study are as follows:

1. It is possible for the Christian, because he is a new creation following His immersion into Christ, to become like Christ.

2. This new creation must be developed in a continual process of renewing the mind—by seeing the picture of the resurrected Christ, developing the picture of the resurrected Christ, and keeping focused on the picture of the resurrected Christ.

3. God's purpose through the ages was to send the Holy Spirit to those who are faithful to Him, so that fellowship with God may be restored, and the faithful may become perfect like their heavenly Father. God communicates this exciting concept, in words such as promise, mystery, glory, and mirror, that we might better understand His purpose. Forgiveness of sin is a vehicle to the indwelling Spirit, and as a key concept of God, must be understood in comprehending the message of the New Testament. The message of the Old Testament is not merely Christ, but Christ in you. In the mirror of the perfect revelation of God—the completed New Testament and the perfect law—we see the image of the resurrected Christ, and in consequence are being transformed into the same image.

4. The Holy Spirit helps the Christian to become perfect, to crucify his flesh. The Spirit leads him that he might be a son of God, and intercedes for the Christian in prayer.

5. Christians are exhorted to be filled with God's Spirit, not to grieve the Spirit, nor quench Him, and to make our bodies our slaves.

6. Life in Jesus is freedom from the old way of thinking. The Christian joyfully does what God wants in a concentrated effort to be like Christ. He believes that God is able to do exceedingly abundantly beyond what he asks or thinks, by the power of the Holy Spirit who works within.

Understanding the concept of the new creation is the central point in understanding Christianity. Only the vision of what we can be in Christ, and a sincere desire to carry out that vision, will give us the motivation to be what God wants us to be. This is what the good news is really all about.

Once again, we remind the reader that the author of this booklet is not inspired, and is subject to error, ignorance, and prejudice. You must go to the Bible itself for answers—all we can do is challenge your thinking.

The New American Standard Version of the Bible was used in preparation of this study, and is quoted throughout.

Your servant,

Jay Wilson

"The Bible only . . . makes Christians only . . ."

the new creation

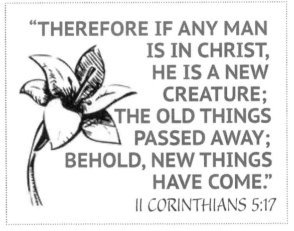

"THEREFORE IF ANY MAN IS IN CHRIST, HE IS A NEW CREATURE; THE OLD THINGS PASSED AWAY; BEHOLD, NEW THINGS HAVE COME."

II CORINTHIANS 5:17

Jay Wilson

THE NEW CREATION

Introduction:

"For neither is circumcision anything, nor uncircumcision, but a new creation" (Galatians 6:15).

I. The Meaning of the New Creation

A. The New Birth
- **II Corinthians 5:17**—For the Christian, all things are new
- **John 3:5; Acts 2:38**—This new beginning occurred in immersion

B. The New Potential
- **Matthew 5:48**—The Christian is to be perfect, as his heavenly Father is perfect
- **Romans 8:29**—The Christian is becoming conformed to the image of Christ
- **I Corinthians 11:1**—The Christian is to be an imitator of Paul, just as he was of Christ
- **I Peter 2:21,22**—Christ left an example for Christians to follow in His steps, who committed no sin

C. The New Picture
- **Matthew 11:11**—the least in the kingdom of heaven (the church) is greater than John the Immerser, the greatest man ever born of human parents
- **John 1:13**—The Christian is greater than John because he is now born of God
- **Romans 6:1–11**—The old man is buried with Christ in immersion. More importantly, the new man is to consider himself as Jesus was when He came out of the tomb!
- **Colossians 3:1–11**—The old self is laid aside, and the new self is being renewed to a true knowledge according to the image of the One who created him
- **Ephesians 4:20–24**—The old self is laid aside, and the new self, which has been created in the likeness of God, is being renewed in the spirit of the mind

It is possible for the Christian, because he is a new creation following his new birth, to become like Christ.

i

II. Developing the New Creature

A. We must believe that we can be like Christ
  - **Isaiah 1:18; Romans 10:17**—God works with our minds
  - **Romans 8:3,4**—Christ came as an offering for sin, and in the likeness of sinful flesh, in order that we might fulfill the requirement of the Law by walking according to the Spirit
  - **Philippians 4:13**—We can do all things through Christ

B. We must set our minds
  - **Romans 8:5–8**—The mind set on the flesh is death, but the mind set on the Spirit is life and peace
    1. Put the church first (Matthew 6:33)
    2. Personally seek and save the lost (Luke 19:10)
    3. Work out the contract of salvation (Philippians 2:12)
    4. Set the mind on things above (Colossians 3:2)

C. Keep focusing the mind on God's things
  - **Romans 12:2**—Be transformed by renewing the mind
  - **Philippians 4:8**—Let the mind dwell on good things
  - Points in Christianity designed to help the Christian keep focusing his mind on things above
    1. The Lord's Supper
    2. The assembly of the saints
    3. Prayer
    4. Study and memorizing of scripture
    5. Singing psalms, hymns, and spiritual songs
    6. Becoming a teacher of God's word
  - **Matthew 12:30**—He who does not gather with Jesus scatters. There are no half–way programs

The new creature is developed by a continual process of renewing the mind. The individual's mind must be persuaded that he can be like Christ, then he must be determined to do so. God helps the Christian to maintain his determination by providing the assistance of the church.

III. God's Purpose

A. Body, soul, and spirit
  - **I Thessalonians 5:23**—The human being is different from animals; being not only body and soul, but also spirit. He has spiritual needs which can be met only by fellowship with God.

B. The promise
- **Galatians 3:22**—All men are shut up under sin, that they might receive the promise through faith in Christ
- **Galatians 3:13,14**—Christ redeemed us from the curse of the Law so that we might receive the promise—the Holy Spirit
- **Ephesians 1:13,14**—We received the Holy Spirit of promise when we listened to the message of truth, the gospel of our salvation
- **Acts 2:38,39**—Immersion in Jesus' name—which grants forgiveness of sins —is so that we might receive the promised Holy Spirit
- **Hebrews 11:39,40**—The great men of faith before Christ did not receive the promise—the Holy Spirit

C. The mystery
- **Colossians 1:24–27**—The mystery which was hidden from the past ages and generations is Christ in you
- **Romans 8:9–11**—Another name for the indwelling Holy Spirit is Christ in you.
- **Genesis 12:3; Galatians 3:13,14**—The blessing of Abraham is a prophecy of the Holy Spirit for the Gentiles
- **Ephesians 3:1–7**—The mystery, which was not revealed to past generations, is that the Gentiles are fellow heirs, fellow members of the body, and fellow partakers of the promise
- **Ephesians 3:8–10**—Paul's purpose was to bring to light the administration of this mystery
- **Colossians 4:3,4**—Paul asked the Colossians to pray for him, that he might make the mystery of Christ clear
- **Ephesians 6:18,19**—Paul asked the Ephesians to pray for him, that he might make known with boldness the mystery of the gospel

D. Glory
- **John 8:54,55**—The state of glory results from being glorified
- **John 7:37–39**—Jesus was not glorified until His resurrection, and the Holy Spirit was not given until that glorification
- **I Timothy 3:16**—Jesus was taken up in glory
- **Isaiah 6:1–10**—Isaiah saw the glory of Yahweh
- **John 12:36–41**—John said that Isaiah saw Jesus' glory
- **Acts 2:29–36**—David as a prophet looked ahead and spoke of the resurrection of the Christ, just as Isaiah did
- **Philippians 3:20,21**—Our bodies will be changed into conformity with the body of His glory
- **I Corinthians 15:42–44**—Our bodies are sown in dishonor, raised in glory

- **Romans 8:18–20**—Our hope is for our bodies to be redeemed—to enter a state of glory
- **Hebrews 9:28**—Jesus is coming for the salvation of the body
- **I Thessalonians 5:8,9**—We have the hope of salvation of the body
- **Romans 8:22–25**—We eagerly await our adoption as sons, the redemption of our bodies
- **Ephesians 1:13,14**—The Holy Spirit is the guarantee of our redemption
- **Colossians 1:27**—Christ in you is called the hope of glory
- **I Peter 4:14**—The Holy Spirit is called the Spirit of glory
- **Titus 2:13**—We look for the blessed hope and appearing of the glory of Jesus
- **Romans 13:11**—Our salvation is now nearer than when we first believed

E. The mirror
- **I Corinthians 13:8–13**—The mirror is the completed New Testament
- **James 1:23–25**—The mirror into which the effectual doer of the word takes an intent look is the perfect law
- **II Corinthians 3:18**—We behold in the mirror the glory of the Lord, and are being transformed into the same image from our present state of glory to the future state of glory

F. Summary and conclusion
- **John 14:23**—Full fellowship with the Father is restored through the Holy Spirit as Father and Son come to live within
- **II Corinthians 4:16**—Even though the outer man is decaying, the inner man is being renewed day by day
- **Titus 3:5,6**—God saves us by the washing of regeneration (immersion) and renewing by the Holy Spirit

>**God's purpose throughout the ages has been to send the Holy Spirit to live in those who love and obey Him. He uses "cipher" words such as *promise*, *mystery*, *glory*, and *mirror* to communicate that purpose. Through the Holy Spirit, fellowship with God, which was lost through Adam, is restored to Christians.**<

IV. What Does The Spirit Do For The Christian?

A. **II Timothy 1:7**—We received the Spirit of power, love, and discipline
B. **Galatians 5:16–25**—He helps the Christian to crucify the flesh and bear the fruit of the Spirit

C. **Romans 8:14**—The Spirit leads us that we may be sons of God
  1. He leads us through the Bible—**John 6:63; II Timothy 3:16,17**
  2. He leads us through our consciences—**I Timothy 1:19; I Corinthians 8:12; I Timothy 4:2; I Corinthians 4:4**
  3. He leads us through events over which we have no control—**Acts 16:7,8; I Corinthians 12:18**

D. The Spirit intercedes for us in prayer—**Romans 8:26,27**

≻⊷We received the same Spirit in our bodies as lived in Jesus—the Spirit of power, love, and discipline. He helps us to crucify the flesh, He leads us that we might be the sons of God, and He intercedes for us in prayer.⊷≺

V. Exhortations From The Spirit

A. Be filled with the Spirit—**Ephesians 5:18**
  1. By singing psalms, hymns, and spiritual songs—**Ephesians 5:19; Matthew 26:30; Acts 16:25**
  2. By giving thanks for all things—**Ephesians 5:20; Joseph in Egypt; Romans 8:28**
  3. By being subject to one another—**Ephesians 5:21; Luke 22:24 and John 13:15; Matthew 20:28; John 15:11**

B. Do not grieve the Spirit
  - **Ephesians 4:30**—Do not grieve the Spirit by carrying out anything which offends Him
  - **Hebrews 6:4–6**—If we grieve Him long enough, we will lose our fellowship with Him—we will be classed as those who were once partakers

C. Do not quench the Spirit—**I Thessalonians 5:19**

D. Making our bodies our slaves—**I Corinthians 9:24–27**

≻⊷The Holy Spirit exhorts us to take more and more control of our own actions, to make our selves subject to His will.⊷≺

VI. Life! in Jesus

  - **John 1:4; John 14:6**—In Jesus is life
  - **Romans 8:2**—The law of the Spirit of life in Christ Jesus has set us free from the law of sin and death
  - **Philippians 3:14**—We are to follow the upward call of God in Christ Jesus

- **I John 5:3,4**—Christ's commandments are not burdensome; we can overcome our wrong attitudes through faith
- **Ephesians 3:20**—God is able to do exceedingly abundantly beyond all that we ask or think—through the Holy Spirit within

➤➤There is joy in living in Christ because we know that God will do great things through us when we commit ourselves to keeping His commandments. God can do more than we can even ask or think through the Holy Spirit who lives in us.◄

Therefore . . .

If any man is in Christ, he is a new creature;

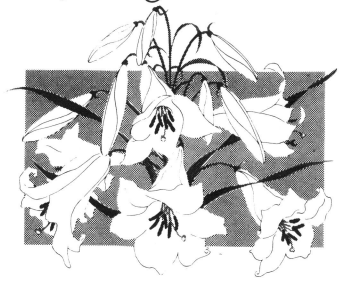

The old things have passed away; behold, new things have come.

2 Corinthians 5:17

THE NEW CREATION

INTRODUCTION

The "good news" of Christianity is not centered on forgiveness of sin. That a lost and damned-to-hell sinner may have forgiveness of sin is certainly good news, but forgiveness of sin obtained through repentance and immersion in Jesus' name is only to take care of the past. Once his past is buried, the Christian's problem is to live today for Christ, spotless and without sin. He must "turn over a new leaf," or as Jesus said it, "You must be born again" (John 3:7). In order to live his new life in Christ, the Christian finds that he needs help. This help is available through the Holy Spirit.

The apostle Paul stated the importance of our subject in this way: "For neither is circumcision anything, nor uncircumcision, but *a new creation*" (Galatians 6:15). The essence of Christianity is found in understanding the new creation. Unless we understand what God envisions us as being, Christianity is nothing more than an extremely burdensome set of rules which are grudgingly obeyed. Such obedience is death.

I. THE MEANING OF THE NEW CREATION
The New Birth

"Therefore if any man is in Christ, he is *a new creature*; the old things passed away; behold, new things have come" (II Corinthians 5:17).

We have seen (in the study entitled *God's Plan of Salvation*) that an individual enters into Christ through immersion in water (Romans 6:3; Galatians 3:27). In immersion—by virtue of being placed into Christ—the individual is now a new creature. In answer to Nicodemus' question about how to be born again, Jesus answered, "Unless one is born of water and the Spirit, he cannot enter into the kingdom of God" (John 3:5). Being born again consists of being born of both water and Spirit, as Peter said on the Day of Pentecost: "Repent, and let each of you be immersed [in *water*— Acts 10:47,48] in the name of Jesus Christ for the forgiveness of your sins, and you shall receive the gift of the *Holy Spirit*" (Acts 2:38). In this new

1

birth, the past is buried with Jesus in immersion (Romans 6:4); but the real importance of the new birth lies not in burying the past, but in sharing in Jesus' resurrection. "Behold, new things have come!" (For more detail on the new birth of water and Spirit, see the study *The Holy Spirit*, the section dealing with the indwelling Holy Spirit.)

What is this new creature? What are the old things that have passed away? And, more importantly, what are the new things that have come?

The New Potential

In the sermon on the mount, Jesus told His followers: "Therefore you are to be perfect, as your heavenly Father is perfect" (Matthew 5:48).

Various weasel-worded explanations have been given in trying to blunt the thrust of Jesus' statement. Some speak of "perfect love" (as if perfect love without perfect behavior were possible) as what Jesus desires. But Jesus is very clear—we are to be perfect (complete, mature) as our heavenly Father is perfect (complete, mature). We are to be like our heavenly Father in every respect.

The same thought is emphasized in the epistles. Paul speaks of our predetermined purpose as becoming "conformed to the image of His Son" (Romans 8:29). "Be imitators of me," he wrote, "just as I also am of Christ" (I Corinthians 11:1). Peter drives the point home in these words: "For you have been called for this purpose, since Christ also suffered for you, leaving you an example for you to follow in His steps, who committed no sin, nor was any deceit found in His mouth" (I Peter 2:21,22). We as Christians are to become conformed to the image of Christ, to be imitators of Christ, and to follow in His steps. In simple terms, we as Christians are to be like Christ.

But is this possible? Has God set for us a task that is impossible to complete? Has He set for us a goal that is impossible to achieve? Has He laid upon us a yoke which neither we nor our fathers could bear?

The answer to these questions, as we shall see, is "No!" God has opened the doorway of perfection to us. But the process of becoming like Christ is much like the process of picture taking. The picture of perfection must be "snapped"—it must be implanted in the film of the brain. Then it must be "developed"—the fleeting snapshot must be developed into a permanent picture. And the picture must be kept constantly in front of us, or it is soon forgotten.

The New Picture

Our first step, then, is to take the picture—to understand that we can be perfect, as our heavenly Father is perfect. How, we ask, can these things be?

We begin with the words of Jesus: "Truly I say to you, among those born of women there has not arisen anyone greater than John the Immerser; yet he who is least in the kingdom of heaven is greater than he" (Matthew 11:11).

John is described by Jesus as the greatest ever born of woman (it will be evident shortly how Jesus exempted Himself from that statement). He is described as "more than a prophet" (Matthew 11:9). To get the full impact of Jesus' point, consider the long list of Old Testament greats. Men such as Abel, Enoch, Abraham, Moses, David, Elijah, Elisha, Isaiah, Zerubbabel, and Zechariah cross our minds. These are those "who by faith conquered kingdoms, performed acts of righteousness, obtained promises, shut the mouths of lions, quenched the power of fire, escaped the edge of the sword, from weakness were made strong, became mighty in war, put foreign armies to flight" (Hebrews 11:34).

That is an impressive list. But John, the last of the Old Testament prophets (the New Testament took effect at the death of Christ—Hebrews 9:16,17), was the greatest of them all. It seems clear that God looked down through the ages and selected the very best to be His forerunner, His messenger to prepare the way for the coming Christ (Matthew 11:10). John was greater than everyone from Abel to Zechariah.

Then Jesus makes this statement: "Yet he who is least in the kingdom of heaven is greater than [John]." What is the kingdom of heaven?

It can be shown from other Scripture that the kingdom of heaven is used interchangeably for the church (see the study entitled *Christ's Church*—the section on the church as the kingdom). For example, in Colossians 1:13, Christians (those delivered from the domain of darkness) are described as already in the kingdom of Christ; the kingdom of Christ is equivalent to the church—which consists of all Christians. A comparison of Matthew 16:28 and its companion Scripture, Mark 9:1, will show that the kingdom of Christ is the same as the kingdom of God. And comparing Matthew 13:11 with Mark 4:11 will show that the kingdom of heaven is the kingdom of God. It is therefore clear that the kingdom of heaven is the kingdom of Christ—the church.

Now back to the statement that the least in the kingdom of heaven is greater than John. What Jesus said was that the *least* Christian is greater than John the Immerser. To bring that into clearer focus: the *least* Christian is greater than Moses, or David or Elijah. The least Christian is greater than everyone from Abel to Zechariah, greater than the greatest born of woman—John the Immerser. Again we—humbly born that we are—ask, how can this be?

In being born of woman, we were born with limited potential. Sin, for example, overpowered us, and we fell short of the glory of God (Romans 3:23). Such is the history of all who are born of woman.

But a hint of God's solution is given in the opening of the gospel of John. When Jesus came into the world, the world which He created did not recognize Him. He came to His own people—Israel—and His own people did not receive Him, but rejected Him. But there were some who recognized Him as the Messiah when He walked in the flesh. Of these it is written: "But as many as received Him, to them He gave the right to become children of God, even to those who believe in His name, who were born not of blood, nor of the will of the flesh, nor of the will of man, but of God" (John 1:12,13). Those who recognized His Messiahship were given the right to become sons of God at some future date—following His resurrection, when the Spirit would be given (see John 7:37–39).

John the Immerser's heritage, greatest though he was of those born of woman, was limited because he was born only of the flesh. But the least Christian is greater than he, for the Christian has been born again—this time not of woman, but *born of God!*

We can now begin to understand why Jesus' command of being perfect is within our reach. In becoming new creatures, we have a new Father, and the limitation of being born of earthly parentage is now shed. (Jesus, in the context of Matthew 11:11, regarded Himself, not as born of woman, but as born of God.)

Dead To Sin

This picture is driven home by the apostle Paul in Romans 6. He first asks the question, "Are we to continue in sin that grace might increase?" The answer obviously is "No!" He then, in two stages, shows us how we can live in the state where we do not sin. Both stages deal with the picture we have of ourselves.

The first picture is that the old man is dead and buried—done away with. "Or do you not know that all of us who have been immersed into Christ Jesus have been immersed *into His death*? Therefore we have been buried with Him through immersion into death, in order that as Christ was raised from the dead through the glory of the Father, so we too might walk in newness of life. For if we have become united with Him in the likeness of His death, certainly we shall be also in the likeness of His resurrection, knowing this, *that our old self was crucified*

with Him, that our body of sin might be done away with, that we should no longer be slaves to sin; for he who has died is freed from sin" (Romans 6:3–7).

Let's visit the morgue (we are dealing with death, remember). Lift the sheet from one of the corpses. Try to tempt him. What images can you flash in front of him that would generate sinful thoughts? What titillating sensations can you use to sway him? What fears can you strike in his heart?

"None," you answer. Why not? You reply, "Because he's dead!"

That is precisely how a Christian is to view himself. In his immersion, the old self was actually crucified, and done away with. The word of the Lord is, "He who has died is freed from sin."

One of the important Biblical principles is that every individual carries out his inner picture of himself. *Self image* is the modern term used to describe this inner picture. The Bible phrases it in this way: "For as he [a man] thinks within himself, so he is" (Proverbs 23:7). As we picture ourselves, so we act. The key to actual change in behavior, then, is to change the inner picture.

In dealing with men, God goes right to the heart of the problem. His first point is to establish that, in one form or another, we view ourselves as failures and act accordingly. "For all have sinned," He says, "and fall short of the glory of God" (Romans 3:23).

But rather than trying to work with the failure—rather than trying to reconstitute or restructure him—God simply buries him. Such is the first picture driven into our minds by the hammer of God's word—"He who has died is freed from sin!" The old things have truly passed away!

Alive To God

In the first seven verses of Romans 6 the apostle Paul is primarily stressing the burial of the old man. In verses 8–11 of the same chapter he now gives us a new picture. "Now if we have died with Christ, we believe that we shall also live with Him, knowing that Christ, having been raised from the dead, is never to die again; *death no longer is master over Him*. For the death that He died, He died to sin, once for all; but the life that He lives, He lives to God" (Romans 6:8–11). In dealing with us, the inspired apostle draws upon the resurrection of Christ.

Jesus in His resurrected state is described as "dead to sin, but alive to God." We ask the question, "How much power did the devil have over Jesus after His resurrection?" The answer, of course, is "No power at all." In raising from the dead, Jesus did "render powerless him who had the power of death, that is , the devil" (Hebrews 2:14). Although the devil could tempt Jesus while He was in the flesh, Jesus—having smashed the devil's head in His resurrection—is now beyond temptation. He now "cannot be tempted by evil, and He Himself does not tempt anyone" (James 1:13). Death truly is no longer master over Him, and in this resurrected state is "dead to sin, and alive to God."

We are now prepared for verse 11, which is specifically written for us. "Even so consider yourselves to be dead to sin, but alive to God in Christ Jesus." When we recall that the words "dead to sin and alive to God" are descriptive of Jesus in His resurrected state, we understand that God has just exhorted us to picture—consider is the word he uses—ourselves as already resurrected! **We are to view ourselves as Jesus was when He came out of the tomb!**

In our immersions, not only did God arrange for the burial of the old man, but more importantly, He arranged for the resurrection of a totally new creature! This new creature—by the command of the Almighty—is to view himself as already resurrected!

The significance of this resurrection cannot be overstressed. A person who views himself as a sinner or failure will continue to act in that way. God's solution to man's problems is to give us self images as those who are beyond the reach of Satan. Only by viewing ourselves in this fashion can we live the life of Christ and not continue in sin. "As a man thinks within himself, so he is."

This is why Paul is so emphatic: "For if we have become united with Him in the likeness of His death, *certainly* we shall be also in the likeness of His resurrection" (Romans 6:5). Just as we participate in the likeness of Jesus' death (immersion) now, so we also participate in the likeness of Jesus' resurrection **now**! If temptation and fear have no effect upon a dead man, how much

**Getting
The
Picture**

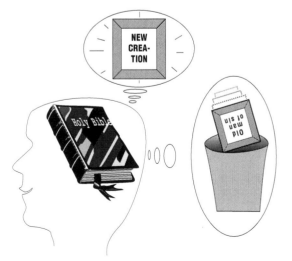

7

less effect do they have on a resurrected man?

These same points are stressed throughout the New Testament. "If then you have been *raised up with Christ*, keep seeking the things above, where Christ is, seated at the right hand of God. Set your mind on the things above, not on the things that are on earth. *For you have died* and your life is hidden with Christ in God. When Christ, who is our life, is revealed, then you also will be revealed with Him in glory. Therefore consider the members of your earthly body as *dead* to immorality, impurity, passion, evil desire, and greed, which amounts to idolatry. For it is on account of these things that the wrath of God will come, and in them you also once walked, when you were living in them. But now, you also, put them all aside: anger, wrath, malice, slander, and abusive speech from your mouth. Do not lie to one another, *since you laid aside the old self* with its evil practices, and *have put on the new self* who is being renewed to a true knowledge according to the image of the One who created him—a renewal in which there is no distinction between Greek and Jew, circumcised and uncircumcised, barbarian, Scythian, slave and freeman, but Christ is all and in all" (Colossians 3:1–11).

"But you did not learn Christ in this way, if indeed you have heard Him and have been taught in Him, just as the truth is in Jesus, that, in reference to your former manner of life, you *lay aside the old self*, which is being corrupted in accordance with the lusts of deceit, and that you be *renewed in the spirit of your mind,*

> **Our picture—what we can be in Christ—is imprinted in our minds like physical pictures:**
>
> * We take the snapshot, the image of the glorified Christ
> * We develop the picture
> * We keep the picture before our eyes

and put on the new self, which in the likeness of God has been created in righteousness and holiness of the truth" (Ephesians 4:20–24).

The new creation has the new potential of being like Christ. The first step in the development of this new potential is a dual new picture—that of the old self being dead, and that of the new self being already resurrected with Christ. It is true—exciting *"new things have come!"*

Summary

It is possible for the Christian, because he is a new creation following his new birth, to become like Christ.

II.   DEVELOPING THE NEW CREATURE
We Must Believe That We Can Be Like Christ

Christianity is somewhere between your eyes and the back of your head. I know that the Bible says that you must "believe in your heart that God raised Jesus from the dead" (Romans 10:9), but the same apostle, in the same epistle, seems very concerned about the "set mind" (Romans 8:5).

The message of God begins with an appeal to the anguished adult: "Come now, let us reason together" says the Lord (Isaiah 1:18). "Faith comes from hearing, and hearing by the word of Christ" (Romans 10:17).

In the same way, the development of the new potential begins with "reasoning together" with God and believing that we can be what He says we can. We must believe that we do have the potential of being like Christ. If we do not believe that we can, it is certain that we won't. Consider carefully the following Scripture:

"For what the Law could not do, weak as it was through the flesh, God did: sending His own Son in the likeness of sinful flesh and as an offering for sin, He condemned sin in the flesh, *in order that the requirement of the Law might be fulfilled in us*, who do not walk according to the flesh, but according to the Spirit" (Romans 8:3,4).

What is the requirement of the Law? Sin is defined as breaking the Law, or lawlessness (I John 3:4). The requirement of the Law is sinlessness, or perfection. Who is going to

For the message of the cross is foolishness to those who are perishing, but to us who are being saved it is the power of God. 1 Corinthians 1:18

fulfill the requirement of the Law? Jesus? The Holy Spirit says that Christians fulfill the requirement of the Law! The Holy Spirit says that Christians are going to live perfect lives by walking according to the Spirit rather than according to the flesh.

The Law (the Old Covenant) could never generate the kind of people who could keep it. But the gospel can generate the kind of people who can be as righteous as the Law required! God did two things which condemned sin in the flesh, and which made it possible for us to meet the requirement of the Law, through the Spirit.

1. **He sent His Son as an offering for sin.** One of the exciting characteristics of God's grace is that Jesus paid the full price for our sins. When a person is immersed into Christ, the past is completely obliterated, as the writer of Hebrews quotes from Jeremiah: "For I will be merciful to their iniquities, and I will remember their sins no more" (Hebrews 8:12).

    One of the important characteristics of this grace is that it is applied, not only to a person's immersion into Christ, but whenever he needs it in his Christian walk. "We have obtained," Paul writes, "our introduction by faith into this grace in which we stand" (Romans 5:2). We need to realize that grace is designed by God for the Christian—there are no other people on the face of the earth who stand in God's good graces. For the older, more mature Christian, as well as for the dripping wet immersee, yesterday is gone. It was nailed to the cross with Christ. He came as an offering for our sins.

    With that bit of good news, however, God also wiped out one of our excuses. "I can't be perfect today," we say, "because I wasn't perfect yesterday."

    What happened to yesterday? It was nailed to the cross with Christ, and with it our sins. But also nailed there was our excuse that we cannot be perfect today because of yesterday. He condemned sin in the flesh by His offering on the cross that we might fulfill the requirement of the Law.

10

2.   **He sent His Son in the likeness of sinful flesh.** When Jesus walked in the flesh, how human was He? In emphasizing the divinity of Jesus Christ, we sometimes forget that He also came as the Son of man, that He "emptied Himself, taking the form of a bondservant, and being made in the likeness of men" (Philippians 2:7). But Jesus was 100% human. He became hungry, He got tired, and He wept. He came in the likeness of sinful flesh.

Did Jesus ever sin? "For we do not have a high priest who cannot sympathize with our weaknesses, but one who has been tempted in all things as we are, yet without sin" (Hebrews 4:15). Jesus was tempted in every way that we are, yet He never yielded to temptation.

Why didn't Jesus sin? Our initial tendency is to respond, "Because He was God." Notice, however, that this answer begs the question of why Jesus didn't sin when He existed in human form. Our answer comes from Paul's letter to the churches of Galatia: "For the flesh sets its desire against the Spirit, and the Spirit against the flesh, for these are in opposition to one another, so that you may not do the things that you please" (Galatians 5:17). Sin occurs when the flesh wins the battle with the spirit—when the flesh does what it pleases. Jesus never sinned because His Spirit did not, for even the smallest fraction of a second, allow His flesh to dictate to His Spirit.

In coming in the likeness of sinful flesh, and being tempted in all points like we and yet without sin, Jesus destroyed our second excuse for not being perfect. Our second excuse is this: "It can't be done." Our excuse is gone—Jesus proved, in the likeness of sinful flesh, that it can be done!

The first point in the development of our new potential is really to believe that we can fulfill the requirement of the Law—that we can be tempted in all points like Jesus and yet not sin. We must believe with Paul: "I can do all things through Him who strengthens me" (Philippians 4:13).

11

We Must Set Our Minds

"For those who are according to the flesh set their minds on the things of the flesh, but those who are according to the Spirit, the things of the Spirit. For the mind set on the flesh is death, *but the mind set on the Spirit is life and peace,* because the mind set on the flesh is hostile toward God; for it does not subject itself to the law of God, for it is not even able to do so; and those who are in the flesh cannot please God" (Romans 8:5–8).

Once we realize that we can be like Jesus and believe that we really have that potential, our next step is to **set our minds** toward being like Him.

Any athlete knows that in order to win a race or ball game, he must first set his mind toward winning. If he does not set his mind—if he is not mentally "up"—he will lose.

So the Bible warns us—the mind set on the flesh is death, but the mind set on the Spirit is life and peace.

What does it mean to set the mind on the things of the Spirit? The whole New Testament is designed to help an individual in these matters—to give him guidelines and instructions as to how to set his mind on the things of the Spirit, and what these things are—"All Scripture is inspired by God and profitable for teaching, for reproof, for correction, for training in righteousness; that the man of God may be adequate, equipped for every good work" (II Timothy 3:16,17). The following Scriptures, however, are especially important in showing us what to set our minds on:

1. "But seek first His kingdom and His righteousness; and all these [material] things shall be added to you" (Matthew 6:33).

   One of the biggest concerns of many Christians is "where is the money going to come from?" Jesus allays our fears by telling us that God will provide. Our main item of business is to seek first the kingdom of God and His righteousness.

   This means that the church comes **first**. That shouldn't surprise us—Jesus died for the church and purchased it with His own blood.

   It is very important to our growing to be like Christ that we **set**

12

our minds to attend every possible church function—Bible school, morning assembly, evening assembly, fellowship dinners, etc.

More important than our attendance at such functions is our attitude toward doing so. Jesus said that it is more blessed to give than to receive (Acts 20:35). We must come with the idea of giving ourselves to encourage "one another to love and to good deeds" (Hebrews 10:24). **We must set our minds** to be givers of life and enthusiasm, rather than "wet blankets and cold water throwers."

2. We must remember that Jesus came to "seek and save that which was lost" (Luke 19:10).

Jesus died on the cross and has left the work of seeking and saving the lost to Christians. Jesus has commissioned us all, through the apostles, to "Go therefore and make disciples of all the nations, immersing them into the name of the Father and the Son and the Holy spirit, teaching them to observe all that I commanded you; and lo, I am with you always, even to the end of the age" (Matthew 28:19,20). Lest any should say that only the apostles were to fulfill the commission, we note that disciples are to continue to be immersed into the name of the Father, Son, and Holy Spirit, even to the end of the age. Fulfilling the commission is something every Christian can do, if only he will.

Jesus has commissioned us to:
   a) Go
   b) Make disciples
   c) Immerse them into the name of the Father, Son, and Spirit
   d) Continue to teach them

We must set our minds toward carrying out each of the four parts of that commission. It is designed to make us like Jesus, as we carry out His purpose of seeking and saving the lost.

3. Paul told the church at Philippi: "Work out your salvation with fear and trembling" (Philippians 2:12).

Salvation is a contract between us and our Master. The terms of the agreement are simple—He agrees to save us from the fires of hell on the day of judgment; and we agree in turn to live every minute of our lives here on earth for Him.

Paul wrote, in explaining this to us: "I have been crucified with Christ; and it is no longer I who live, but Christ lives in me" (Galatians 2:20).

Jesus expressed the same concept: "If anyone wishes to come after Me, let him deny himself, and take up his cross daily, and follow Me. For whoever wishes to save his life shall lose it, but whoever loses his life for My sake, he is the one who will save it. For what is a man profited if he gains the whole world and loses or forfeits himself [his soul]?" (Luke 9:23–25).

We must set our minds to working out our contract of salvation. The terms of the contract are guaranteed to make us like Jesus.

4.   In becoming like Jesus, as we labor and strive here on earth, it is possible for a person to become discouraged if he focuses his attention in the wrong direction. A person can be disappointed in himself for failing to be like Jesus, and he can be disappointed in others for failing to receive the message of salvation.

We must recognize that Jesus walked this earthly pilgrimage before us, that He faced every problem that we do, and that He overcame. They hated Him (John 15:25), rejected His message (John 6:60), and killed Him.

But we must follow the inspired advice of Paul in focusing our attention in the proper direction: "*Set your mind* on the things above, not on the things that are on earth" (Colossians 3:2).

A Christian must **recognize** that he has the potential of being like Christ. He must then **believe** that he really can be like Christ. Then he must **set his mind** toward achieving that goal.

The Christian sets his mind on being like Christ by setting his mind on the things of the Spirit. These include:

14

1. Putting the church first.
2. Personally seeking and saving the lost.
3. Working out the contract of salvation.
4. Setting the mind on things above.

Keep Focusing The Mind On God's Things

Once the Christian has set his mind to be like Christ, he faces another problem—the tendency to lose his resolve.

We are warned against such loss of resolve: "And do not be conformed to this world, but be transformed by *the renewing of your mind*, that you may prove [test] what the will of God is, that which is good and acceptable and perfect" (Romans 12:2).

Again, the Spirit says, "Finally, brethren, whatever is true, whatever is honorable, whatever is right, whatever is pure, whatever is lovely, whatever is of good repute, if there is any excellence and if anything worthy of praise, *let your mind dwell on these things*" (Philippians 4:8).

The mind is in constant need of renewal. The only way to be transformed or changed is by the process of renewing or reprogramming the mind. Many people pray for God to change them—God has told us how to be changed: *Renew the mind!* Failure to reprogram the mind will result in a person's being conformed to this world.

It is extremely important that the Christian control his mental environment. Outer actions are the reflection of inner attitudes. That is why the Holy Spirit has exhorted us to make sure our minds dwell—live—on excellent thoughts.

We also need practical ways to keep our minds focused on Christ. God has so designed the church that all the basic activities of Christianity are perfect for the purpose of helping us keep our minds set!

1. The Lord's Supper is one of the most important practices in keeping our minds set on being like Christ. The night in which Jesus was betrayed, He took both the bread and the cup (which was filled with juice from the fruit of the vine) and of both He said, "do this

in remembrance of Me'" (I Corinthians 11:24,25).

The early church participated in the Lord's Supper (which they also called "the breaking of bread"—I Corinthians 10:16) every first day of the week as their primary purpose for meeting together (Acts 20:7). The remembrance of Jesus is central in our purpose for meeting together—we should be motivated by that remembrance!

The importance of the Supper is stated this way by Jesus: "Unless you eat the flesh of the Son of Man and drink His blood, you have no life in yourselves" (John 6:53). Isn't that what we want—*life?*

2. The assembly of the saints is designed to help us keep our attention focused on being like Christ. As Jesus went about doing good (Acts 10:38), so we are to "consider how to stimulate on another to love and good deeds" (Hebrews 10:24).

    God knows the value of teamwork and the mutual encouragement that arises when a good team works toward the same goal. For this reason "God has placed the members, each one of them, in the body, just as He desired" (I Corinthians 12:18).

    Working with the local church should not be a drudgery—rather it should be a joy to meet with and work at helping each other to become like Christ.

3. Prayer is also designed to focus our attention on being new creatures. Notice how carefully God works with our attitudes and desires before He consents to answer:

    a) He answers prayers in Jesus' name (John 14:14). This again draws our attention to the fact that we cannot come to God on our own, but only through Him who died that we might become like Him.

    b) He also works with our attitude in really believing. "And all things you ask in prayer, *believing*, you shall receive" (Matthew 21:22). This again triggers the thought in our minds that we must not only recognize the potential we have in Christ, we must really work with our belief level in every respect!

c) Prayer also works with our inner motives. "You ask and do not receive, because you ask with wrong motives, so that you may spend it on your pleasures" (James 4:3). Are our inner motives to be like Jesus and to work for the spread and growth of His kingdom?

d) God uses prayer to develop persistence within us. "Now He was telling them a parable to show that at all times they ought to pray and not to lose heart" (Luke 18:1). Jesus was in constant fellowship with the Father in prayer; yet the Father did not always answer His prayers the way His natural desires would have them answered: "My Father, if it is possible, let this cup pass from Me; yet not as I will, but as You will" (Matthew 26:39). This persistence and submission to the will of the Father makes it possible for us to carry our crosses down the way of life in the footsteps of Jesus.

4. Studying and memorizing the Scripture is also very important to the formation of the new creation. Paul wrote that it is "the word of God which also performs its work in you who believe" (I Thessalonians 2:13). Jesus said, "The words that I have spoken to you are spirit and are life" (John 6:63).

The only way to be transformed is by "the renewing of the mind" (Romans 12:2). The best way to be renewed is to be continually working in God's word. His thoughts can never become our thoughts unless we read and become familiar with the Bible.

Mere reading and studying the Bible will not do the job. Sooner or later we must all realize that in order to become like our Lord we must memorize it. Recall how Jesus answered the devil in the wilderness (Matthew 4:1–11)—with memorized Scripture! Even at the age of twelve He amazed the doctors of the Law with His knowledge and grasp of God's word. Part of Jesus' being human is that it was no easier for Him to memorize the Scriptures than it is for us. Let's go to work.

Jesus stressed the importance of having the Scripture memorized in this way, "If you abide in Me, and My words abide in you, ask whatever you wish, and it shall be done for you" (John 15:7). Or does a man live by bread alone?

5. Singing psalms and hymns and spiritual songs is part of developing to be like Jesus. Colossians 3:16 makes it clear that such singing is a way of teaching and admonishing one another and of letting the word of Christ richly dwell within us. Ephesians 5:19 points out that this is the way of being filled with God's Spirit.

6. Becoming a teacher of God's word is an effective means of being transformed. A principle of which we are all aware is that we have not really learned anything well until we have reached the point at which we can teach others. The repetition, the answering of questions, the enthusiasm required to spark others' interest, and the hard work of preparation all make us more like Him who was known as the Teacher (John 13:14).

In becoming teachers, James warns us: "Let not many of you become teachers, my brethren, knowing that as such we shall incur a stricter judgment" (James 3:1). We are encouraged to become teachers (Hebrews 5:12), but we are cautioned that we don't move too fast, for the teacher is responsible to God for what he says, and he must always be accurate in his handling of the word of truth.

God wants us to commit ourselves to disciplining our thinking, that we might become like Jesus. He has given the church various activities designed to help us focus and keep concentrating our attention on His Son and that we might continue to enthusiastically press on.

It is plain that keeping our minds on the things of the Spirit requires driving dedication and humble desire. There are no half-way programs, no short-cut ways to becoming the new creatures that we can be. It's all or nothing, as Jesus said, "He who is not with Me is against Me . . ." (Matthew 12:30). Let's press on in working out our contract with enthusiasm!

Summary

The new creature is developed by a continual process of renewing the mind. The individual's mind must be persuaded that he can be like Christ, then he must be determined to do so. God helps the Christian to maintain his determination by providing the assistance of the church.

III.   GOD'S PURPOSE

Body, Soul, And Spirit

"Now may the God of peace Himself sanctify you entirely; and may your spirit and soul and body be preserved complete, without blame at the coming of our Lord Jesus Christ" (I Thessalonians 5:23).

The human being consists of three parts—body, soul, and spirit.

1.   The body is that physical part of us referred to in the Bible as "the flesh" (Galatians 5:16) and our "earthly tent" (II Corinthians 5:1). It is our temporary home, and is not the real "us"—it is only the place in which the real person lives while on earth.

2.   The soul is the "living" part of us. It is the soul which sees, feels, hears, and thinks—forever!

Physical death is the separation of the soul from the body (see Acts 2:27). Though the body is dead—though the eyes no longer see, for example—the soul continues to see in Hades (the temporary resting place for the souls of the dead). In Luke 16:23 the rich man is described as "in Hades he lifted up his eyes"—a figure of speech meaning that he continued to see.

The soul is the life of the human being. When the soul leaves, the eyes no longer see and the ears no longer hear. The eyes and ears were merely physical means through which the soul operated while on earth.

19

3.   The spirit is the deep inner part of a person. When God made man in His image (Genesis 1:26), He made him a spirit being. Since God is Spirit (John 4:24), neither the physical part of man, nor his soul, is in the image of God. It is in being a spirit that man is made in God's image.

It is in being a spirit that distinguishes man from animals. Animals are body and soul, but not spirit. In being a spirit, man is a moral being. He is not to operate by instinct as unreasoning animals do (see II Peter 2:12), but he has a choice of doing right or wrong.

This spiritual part of man might be described as his will—his desire to press on—his desire for deep fellowship.

The Promise Of The Spirit

Sometimes God, in His inspired word, uses words with special emphasis or meaning which can be derived only by a study of those words in their contexts. I call them "cipher" words or "code" words. Once the meaning of a "cipher" word is understood, then the message of the passage in which it is used can be "deciphered." If the meaning of the "cipher" word is not understood, then the main thrust of that passage of Scripture is lost upon the student of God's word.

One such "cipher" word is promise. Sometimes promise refers to eternal life (I John 2:25). Promises, for example in II Peter 1:4, talks about many blessings found in Jesus Christ as revealed in the New Testament. But what we want to show is that *the promise*, when it stands alone, is generally a reference to the indwelling presence of the Holy Spirit (why it has to be the indwelling Spirit rather than the immersion in the Spirit or the gifts is clear from the study entitled *The Holy Spirit*). And then, with that key of understanding, we want to unlock some very important conceptual doors of the New Covenant.

In his letter to the Galatians, the apostle Paul writes: "But the Scripture has shut up all men under sin, that *the promise* by faith in Jesus Christ might be given to those who believe" (Galatians 3:22). What he calls the promise—which comes by faith in Jesus—is so important that God shut up

20

all men in the jail house of sin so that they might receive it. In other words, the reason for God's binding men under sin is so that they might receive this promise. The important question is: What is *the promise*?

Earlier in this same letter, the apostle defined the promise for us. "Christ redeemed us from the curse of the Law, having become a curse for us—for it is written, 'Cursed is everyone who hangs on a tree'—in order that in Christ Jesus the blessing of Abraham might come to the Gentiles, so that we might receive the promise *of the Spirit* through faith" (Galatians 3:13,14). The promise is the Spirit, in the same way as in Acts 2:38, where the gift is the Spirit. Paul emphasizes the same point in his letter to the Ephesians: "In Him, you also, after listening to the message of truth, the gospel of your salvation—having also believed, you were sealed in Him with the *Holy Spirit of promise*, who is given as a pledge of our inheritance, with a view to the redemption of God's own possession, to the praise of His glory" (Ephesians 1:13,14). The Holy Spirit is the promise!

Having defined our "cipher" word, we can now decipher the message of Galatians 3, and discover there an extremely important foundational point of the New Covenant. It is clear from Galatians 3:22 that God's reason for shutting us up under sin is so that we might receive the promise. The same point is clear in Galatians 3:13,14. He says, "Christ redeemed us," and then he says, "in order that." Redemption—salvation, or forgiveness of sins—is for another purpose. What is that other purpose?

The importance of purpose can be illustrated in this way. Suppose you drive your car downtown "in order" to buy groceries. Notice that your purpose is to buy groceries—the automobile is simply the vehicle you have chosen to get you there.

God's purpose is expressed in these words: "in order that" the blessing of Abraham might come; that is, that we might receive the promise of the Holy Spirit. The purpose is the promise of the Spirit.

Note, then, that forgiveness of sins—redemption—is simply the vehicle God has chosen to carry out His purpose.

That forgiveness of sins is the vehicle, and that God's purpose is the indwelling Holy Spirit has two very important corollaries. The first is that the central message of the New Testament is not forgiveness of sins. Forgiveness of sins is a very important vehicle—and it's wonderful that forgiveness of sins can be obtained through Christ our Savior—but the vehicle is always subordinate to the purpose. When forgiveness of sins is the central focus of preaching, that preaching misses the mark of the New Testament. Forgiveness of sins must first be preached to the lost—that is the only message that carnal man first understands. But following immersion, the Christian's attention must be turned from the "have to" of the Law to the "want to" of perfection offered through the Spirit. Understanding that forgiveness is the vehicle, and that the promise of the Spirit is God's purpose is the difference between life and death, and the difference between the Law and the Faith!

The second corollary deals with the importance of the indwelling of God's Spirit. God first deals with men on the plane of their guilty consciences and forgiveness which He offers. The fleshly mind apparently cannot grasp the significance of the indwelling Spirit, so to move men's understanding to the proper point, God uses the Scripture to shut us in the jail house of sin. (Being shut up in a jail house is a drastic measure, but it is the only one which communicates.) Having been locked up, and having recognized our condition, we are now ready to listen to the voice of the Almighty.

In recognizing how important forgiveness of sins is—the difference between glory in heaven and eternity in the lake of fire—and understanding that forgiveness is the vehicle to a more important purpose, we now understand how important the promise of the Spirit is. This is God's way of communicating to a still groggy—but awakening—mind the significance of His indwelling Spirit. "Awake, sleeper, and arise from the dead, and Christ will shine on you" (Ephesians 5:14).

The central message of the New Testament is the promise—the indwelling Holy Spirit!

Listen, then, to the inspired words of Peter on the day of Pentecost, 30

22

A.D. "Repent," he says in proclaiming for the first time in the history of the world the terms of the New Covenant, "and let each of you be immersed in the name of Jesus Christ for the forgiveness of your sins; and you shall receive the gift of the Holy Spirit. For *the promise* is for you and your children, and for all who are far off, as many as the Lord our God shall call to Himself" (Acts 2:38,39).

The thrust of Peter's reply was not forgiveness of sins—although forgiveness of sins is involved. The driving point of his answer was **the promise!** Forgiveness of sins is clearly here the vehicle to the promised gift of the Spirit.

Note too those to whom the promise was made. The promise was for "you and your children," an Hebraic expression for the Jews. But the promised Spirit was also for the Gentiles (Peter himself would not understand his own words for another ten years until he preached to the Gentile soldier Cornelius)—"for all who are far off." Paul defines this term for us in explaining the Jew–Gentile relationship in Christ to the Ephesians: "And He came and preached peace to you who were far away, and peace to those who were near; for through Him we both have our access in one Spirit to the Father" (Ephesians 2:17,18). The promise, then, from the day of Pentecost onward, was to be for both Jew and Gentile!

Now we are ready to examine a very important statement by the author of Hebrews. "And all these [the Old Testament great men of faith], having gained approval through their faith, did not receive *what was promised* [literally, *the promise*!], because God had provided something [Someone] better for us, so that apart from us they should not be made perfect" (Hebrews 11:39,40).

We recall that Jesus had said that the least Christian would be greater than John the Immerser (Matthew 11:11). We also established that John was the greatest of all the Old Testament greats, and from that drew the conclusion that the least in the kingdom of heaven was greater than all the Old Testament greats. We asked the question, "How can that be?" and came to the conclusion that the least Christian had been born of God, whereas none of the Old Testament greats—including John—were able to be born again of water and Spirit. The writer of Hebrews makes the same point—all those who died in faith did not receive *the promise*! They were never born of *the*

23

Spirit. The least of us can be greater than any of those in the Old Testament because we are indwelt by God's Spirit!

The central message of the New Testament is the promised Holy Spirit. Those who have received that promise can exceed what any of those in the Old Testament were able to accomplish.

The Mystery

Another "cipher" word is *mystery*. A mystery is a secret, or more specifically, a mental puzzle in which the pieces have been hidden earlier, and then put together in the final chapter.

Like *promise*, the word *mystery* sometimes is used in different ways. For example, the apostle Paul speaks of "the mystery of lawlessness" which was already at work (II Thessalonians 2:7). But God uses the term *the mystery* for a special purpose.

Paul tells us in straight forward fashion what the mystery is, although it is easy to stumble over the importance of his definition. "Now I rejoice in my sufferings for your sake, and in my flesh I do my share on behalf of His body (which is the church) in filling up that which is lacking in Christ's afflictions. Of this church I was made a minister according to the stewardship from God bestowed on me for your benefit, that I might fully carry out the preaching of the word of God, that is, *the mystery* which has been hidden from the past ages and generations; but has now been manifested to His saints, to whom God willed to make known what is the riches of the glory of this *mystery* among the Gentiles, *which is Christ in you*, the hope of glory" (Colossians 1:24–27).

The apostle tells us that the mystery—which was hidden from the past ages and generations—is "Christ in you." What is Christ in you?

We recall the words of Paul to the Romans: "However, you are not in the flesh but in the *Spirit*, if indeed the *Spirit of God* dwells in you. But if anyone does not have the *Spirit of Christ*, he does not belong to Him. And if *Christ is in you*, though the body is dead because of sin, yet the spirit is alive because of righteousness. But if the *Spirit of Him who raised Jesus from the dead* dwells in you, He who raised Christ Jesus from the dead will also give life to your mortal bodies through *His Spirit who indwells you*" (Romans 8:9–11).

Note the names given to the Holy Spirit in this passage:

The Spirit

The Spirit of God

The Spirit of Christ

Christ in you

The Spirit of Him who raised Jesus from the dead

His Spirit who indwells you

Another name for the Holy Spirit is *Christ in you!* **The mystery is the same as the promise—the indwelling Holy Spirit!**

In order to fully carry out the preaching of the word of God, we must understand and preach the mystery. We cannot claim to have restored New Testament Christianity unless the mystery is at the center of our preaching, and we are making known the riches of the glory of this mystery among our present–day Gentiles.

The apostle said that the mystery was hidden from the past ages and generations. Where were the pieces of this mystery hidden? They were hidden in the pages of the Old Testament, and revealed to us by the holy apostles and prophets in the pages of the New. Let's examine one of the pieces of this mystery, and note how carefully it was hidden in the Old Testament, and note as well how easy it is to miss how it is revealed in the New Testament.

Way back in the early stages of God's revelation to man, He blessed Abraham (while he was still Abram). He said, "And I will bless those who bless you, and the one who curses you I will curse. *And in you all the families of the earth will be blessed*" (Genesis 12:3).

Does that look like a prophecy of the Holy Spirit? Look closely, because it is.

Genesis 12:3 is commonly thought to be a prophecy of Christ. Through Abraham Christ would come—not for just the Israelites, but for all nations. But Christ in the flesh only was sent to the lost sheep of the house of Israel.

But let Paul explain: "Christ redeemed us from the curse of the Law, having become a curse for us—for it is written, 'Cursed is everyone who hangs on a tree'—in order that in Christ Jesus *the blessing of Abraham* might come to the Gentiles, so that we might receive the promise of the Spirit through faith" (Galatians 3:13,14).

There are only two valid possibilities as to what *the blessing of Abraham* is. One possibility is salvation; the other possibility is the Holy Spirit. It is easy to eliminate salvation as a possibility, because in verse 13 he says, "Christ redeemed [saved] us," and verse 14 says, "in order that." The blessing of Abraham is the promised Holy Spirit.

The prophecy of Genesis 12:3 is fulfilled—in the Spirit, Christ has blessed all the families of the earth!

There are many other examples of pieces of the mystery hidden in the Old Testament. Our point here, however, is that the message of the Old Testament is not simply Christ. In fact, if the Old Testament were boiled down to one drop of pure elixir, the name of that drop would have to be *The Mystery*.

The message of the Old Testament is not simply Christ, but **Christ in you**!

To some, that distinction may seem like a minor point. But the difference between *Christ* and *Christ in you* is somewhat like leaving the football at the ten-yard line and thinking that you have scored a touchdown. The message of the Old Testament is *Christ in you*, and that is another of God's ways of communicating to a still groggy—but awakening—mind the importance of His indwelling Spirit!

Listen again to the apostle to the Gentiles as he ties together for us the promise and the mystery in writing to the church in Ephesus. "For this reason I, Paul, the prisoner of Jesus Christ for the sake of you Gentiles—if indeed you have heard of the stewardship of God's grace which was given to me for you; that by revelation there was made known to me the mystery, as I wrote before in brief. And by referring to this, when you read you can understand my insight into the mystery of Christ, which in other generations was not made known to the sons of men, as it has now been revealed to His holy apostles and prophets in the Spirit; to be specific, that the Gentiles are fellow heirs and fellow members of the body, and fellow partakers of the promise in Christ Jesus through the gospel, of which I was made a minister, according to the gift of God's grace which was given to me according to the working of His power" (Ephesians 3:1–7).

Notice that here Paul defines as the mystery that the Gentiles are fellow heirs, fellow members of the body, and fellow partakers of the promise. This dovetails perfectly with his definition in Colossians 1:27 that the mystery is Christ in you. Here, by being a fellow partaker of the promise—the Holy Spirit—a Christian is a fellow heir and fellow member of the body. What was hidden from the past ages and generations was made known through the apostles and New Testament prophets, and recorded for us in the foundational New Testament Scriptures!

The mystery—Christ in you, the indwelling Holy Spirit, the promise—is the culmination of God's plan for the duration of the earth. "To me, the very least of all saints, this grace was given, to preach to the Gentiles the unfathomable riches of Christ, and to bring to light what is the *administration of the mystery* which for ages has been hidden in God, who created all things; in order that the manifold wisdom of God might now be made known through the church to the rulers and the authorities in the heavenly places" (Ephesians 3:8–10).

In our teaching and preaching, as imitators of Paul, what is to be our emphasis? "Devote yourselves to prayer, keeping alert in it with an attitude of thanksgiving; praying for us as well, that God may open up to us a door for the word, so that we may speak forth *the mystery* of Christ, for which also I have been imprisoned; in order that I may make it clear in the way I ought to speak" (Colossians 4:2–4)! "Pray on my behalf, that utterance may be given to me in the opening of my mouth, to make known with boldness *the mystery* of the gospel, for which I am an ambassador in chains; that in proclaiming it I may speak boldly, as I ought to speak" (Ephesians 6:19,20)!

The mystery of the gospel—the pieces of which were hidden in the Old Testament Scriptures—is Christ in you, the promised Holy Spirit. The message of the Old Testament, as well as the New, is this mystery and promise. This mystery is to be proclaimed clearly and boldly, that the manifold wisdom of God might be made known to the rulers and authorities in the heavenlies.

Glory

Our next "cipher" word is *glory*. "Glory" is a word that is commonly used, in contrast to "mystery" and "promise." But its real meaning is only vaguely understood. We want to focus in on the specific concept which "glory" represents, and thus open more exciting doors into the unfathomable riches of Christ. What we want to show is that "glory" is a description of the resurrected state, and any meaning of "glory" as "shining" or "elevated" is derived from that.

In a heated discussion with the Jews, Jesus said, "If I *glorify* Myself, My *glory* is nothing; it is my Father who *glorifies* Me, of whom you say, 'He is our God;' and you have not come to know Him, but I know Him; and if I say that I do not know Him, I shall be a liar like you, but I do know Him, and keep His word" (John 8:54,55). Our point here is an obvious one— that in order for Jesus to enter a state of glory He had to be glorified, to be resurrected to unapproachable light.

The apostle John describes an earlier event, when Jesus was at the temple for the feast of tabernacles: "Now on the last day, the great day of the feast, Jesus stood and cried out, saying, 'If any man is thirsty, let him come to Me and drink. He who believes in Me, as the Scripture said, "From his innermost being shall flow rivers of living water." ' " John then explains what Jesus is talking about: "But this He spoke of the Spirit*, whom those who believed in Him were to receive: for the Spirit was not yet given, because *Jesus was not yet glorified*" (John 7:37–39). Jesus was glorified in His resurrection; then the Holy Spirit came on the day of Pentecost. "He who was revealed in the flesh, was vindicated in the Spirit, beheld by angels, proclaimed among the nations believed on in the world, *taken up in glory*" (I Timothy 3:16).

The resurrection and glorification of Christ is the most significant event of history, the proof that God's word is sure, and the anchor for the soul. One example from the Old Testament is necessary here to illustrate the significance of Jesus' resurrection, and the meaning of glory.

"In the year of King Uzziah's death, I saw the Lord sitting on a throne, lofty and exalted, with the train of His robe filling the temple. Seraphim stood above Him, each having six wings; with two he covered his face, and with two he covered his feet, and with two he flew. And one called out to

---

* Here is another piece of the mystery. John tells us that the rivers of living water, referred to by Jesus as from Old Testament scriptures, is another name for the Holy Spirit. To check the Old Testament references for the pieces of the mystery, see Zechariah 14:8 and Ezekiel 47:1-12.

another and said, 'Holy, Holy, Holy, is the LORD of Hosts, the whole earth is full of His *glory*.' And the foundations of the thresholds trembled at the voice of him who called, while the temple was filling with smoke.

"Then I said, 'Woe is me, for I am ruined! Because I am a man of unclean lips; for my eyes have seen the King, the LORD of Hosts.' " (Isaiah 6:1–5).

The word spelled *Lord* is the Hebrew word *adonai*, which means master. The word spelled *LORD* is the tetragrammeton *YHWH*, which is usually pronounced *Yahweh* or *Jehovah*.

We are now prepared to ask, "Whose glory was it that Isaiah saw?" The answer: The LORD—*Yahweh* or *Jehovah*—of Hosts!

Let's continue with this passage from Isaiah for a few more verses: "Then one of the seraphim flew to me, with a coal in his hand which he had taken from the altar with tongs. And he touched my mouth with it and said, 'Behold, this has touched your lips; and your iniquity is taken away; and your sin is forgiven.'

"Then I heard the voice of the Lord, saying, 'Whom shall I send, and who will go for Us?' Then I said, 'Here am I. Send me!'

"And He said, 'Go, and tell this people: "Keep on listening, but do not perceive; keep on looking, but do not understand." Render the hearts of this people insensitive, their ears dull, and their eyes dim, lest they see with their eyes, hear with their ears, understand with their hearts, and return and be healed.' " (Isaiah 6:6–10). Remember what the LORD told Isaiah.

Now we turn to the writings of the apostle John: "These things Jesus spoke, and He departed and hid Himself from them. But though He had performed so many signs before them, yet they were not believing in Him; that the word of Isaiah the prophet might be fulfilled, which he spoke, 'Lord, who has believed our report? And to whom has the arm of the Lord been revealed?' For this cause they could not believe, for Isaiah said again, 'He has blinded their eyes, and He hardened their heart; lest they see with their eyes, and perceive with their heart, and be converted and I heal them.' These things Isaiah said, because *he saw His [Jesus'] glory*, and he spoke of Him" (John 12:36b–41).

Note that John 12:40 is the quotation of Isaiah 6:10. We now ask, "Whose glory was it that Isaiah saw?" The answer: "Jesus'."

The fact that it was Jesus' glory that Isaiah saw makes two things clear. The first is that Jesus is Yahweh (or Jehovah). The second is that what Isaiah saw was Jesus in His resurrected state.

What Isaiah saw was the glory of Jesus as He was seated on the throne. Listen to Peter explain a prophecy of David's, and make the application to the throne which Isaiah saw. "Brethren, I may confidently say to you regarding the patriarch David that he both died and was buried, and his tomb is with us to this day. And so, *because he was a prophet*, and knew that

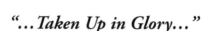

"...Taken Up in Glory..."

God had sworn to him with an oath to seat one of his descendants *upon this throne*, he looked ahead and spoke of *the resurrection of the Christ*, that He was neither abandoned to Hades, nor did His flesh suffer decay. This Jesus God raised up again, to which we are all witnesses. Therefore having been exalted to the right hand of God, and having received from the Father the promise of the Holy Spirit, He has poured forth this which you both see and hear. For it was not David who ascended into heaven, but he himself says: 'The Lord said to my Lord, "Sit at My right hand, until I make your enemies a footstool for your feet." ' Therefore let all the house of Israel know for certain that God has made Him both *Lord* and Christ—this Jesus whom you crucified" (Acts 2:29–36).

Jesus is declared to be both Lord (Yahweh) and Christ (King) by His resurrection! And that is precisely whom Isaiah saw—the King, Yahweh of Hosts, on the throne!

With this clear picture of glory etched in our minds, it is easier to visualize what Moses saw when the glory of the Lord passed by, or what Solomon saw when the glory of the Lord filled the temple. We also understand what it means to glorify or exalt the Lord, as Jesus said, "By this is My Father glorified, that you bear much fruit, and so prove to be My disciples" (John 15:8).

Glory, then, is a description of the resurrected state. "For our citizenship is in heaven, from which we also eagerly wait for a Savior, the Lord Jesus Christ; who will transform the body of our humble state into conformity with *the body of His glory*, by the exertion of the power that He has even to subject all things to Himself" (Philippians 3:20,21). "So also is the resurrection of the dead. It is sown a perishable body, it is raised an imperishable body; it is sown in dishonor, it is raised in *glory*; it is sown in weakness, it is raised in power; it is sown a natural body, it is raised a spiritual body. If there is a natural body, there is also a spiritual body" (I Corinthians 15:42–44).

The desire to be resurrected—the desire for glory—is the driving hope of the Christian. "For I consider that the sufferings of this present time are not worthy to be compared with the *glory* that is to be revealed to us. For the anxious longing of the creation waits eagerly for the revealing of the sons of God. For the creation was subjected to futility, not of its own will, but because of Him who subjected it, in hope that the creation itself will also be set free from its slavery to corruption into the freedom of the *glory* of the children of God" (Romans 8:18–21).

This state of glory is called the salvation, or redemption, of the body. Salvation in the Old Testament meant deliverance from the physical enemy. For example, when Moses prepared to open the Red Sea to save Israel from the chariots of Pharaoh, he said, "Stand by and see the *salvation* of the Lord" (Exodus 14:13). With this concept, it is easy to see how they would misunderstand the prophecies of the coming Savior, Redeemer, or Deliverer of Israel. With the inauguration of the new and living way accomplished through Jesus' death, there was a shift in emphasis. Christians are spoken of as "saved" (Titus 3:5), "redeemed" (Galatians 3:13), and "delivered" (Colossians 1:13). Our souls are "saved," redeemed," and "delivered." But there is a salvation, or redemption, which we yet await.

Of Jesus' second coming, the writer of Hebrews states: "Christ also, having been offered once to bear the sins of many, shall appear a second time *for salvation* without reference to sin, to those who eagerly await Him" (Hebrews 9:28). If Christians are already saved, why is Jesus coming a second time *for salvation*? Or, as Paul wrote to the Thessalonians: "But since we are of the day, let us be sober, having put on the breastplate of faith and love, and as a helmet, *the hope of salvation*. For God has not destined us for wrath, but for *obtaining salvation* through our Lord Jesus Christ" (I Thessalonians 5:8,9).

The hope of salvation which we have—the salvation which we await—is the redemption of the body. "For we know that the whole creation groans and suffers the pains of childbirth together until now. And not only this, but also we ourselves, having the first–fruits of the Spirit, even we ourselves groan within ourselves, waiting eagerly for our adoption as sons, *the redemption of our body*. For in hope we have been saved, but hope that is seen is not hope; for why does one also hope for what he sees? But if we hope for what we do not see, with perseverance we wait eagerly for it" (Romans 8:22–25).

The guarantee that our bodies will be redeemed is the indwelling Holy Spirit. "In Him, you also, after listening to the message of truth, the gospel of your salvation—having also believed, you were sealed in Him with the Holy Spirit of promise, who is given as a *pledge* of our inheritance, with a view to the *redemption of God's own possession*, to the praise of His glory" (Ephesians 1:13,14). Our bodies, which are the temple of the Holy Spirit, are the possession of God, which He will redeem at Christ's coming. Because our redemption is our earnest desire, and because this redemption is guaranteed by the Holy Spirit, the mystery—Christ in you—is called the *hope of glory*! (Colossians 1:27). "If you are reviled for the name of Christ, you are blessed, because *the Spirit of glory* and of God rests upon you" (I Peter 4:14).

As we look "for the blessed hope and appearing of the *glory* of our great God and Savior, Christ Jesus" (Titus 2:13), we are to view ourselves as already resurrected, as those whose citizenship is in heaven, as those who are already seated at the right hand of the throne of God, as already in a state of glory. As we do so, we will be conscious that "now our salvation is nearer to us than when we [first] believed" (Romans 13:11).

Glory is a description of the resurrected state. The Holy Spirit within is our hope of glory, as the guarantee that God will redeem our bodies.

The Mirror

Our last "cipher" word is *mirror*. In examining the passages connected with *the mirror* we will be able to tie up in one neat package the purpose of God.

"Love never fails; but if there are gifts of prophecy, they will be done away; if there are tongues, they will cease; if there is knowledge, it will be done away. For we know in part, and we prophesy in part; but when the perfect comes, the partial will be done away. When I was a child, I used to speak as a child, think as a child, reason as a child; when I became a man, I did away with childish things. For now we see in a *mirror* dimly, but then face to face; now I know in part, but then I shall know fully just as I also have been fully known. But now abide faith, hope, love, these three; but the greatest of these is love" (I Corinthians 13:8–13).

We established in an earlier study (*The Holy Spirit*, the section on the duration of the gifts) that the partial that will be done away are the gifts of the Spirit, such as prophecy, tongues, gift of knowledge. The perfect, or complete, in contrast to the partial that will be done away, is the completed New Testament. In the absence of the completed word, the church in its infancy had to resort to the "childish"—the gifts—in order to function. But in coming to maturity with the written word, the childish could be done away.

Paul and the Corinthians could only see in the *mirror* dimly, but those who would come later would be able to see as if face to face. Paul could only know in part, but those who would come later would be able to know fully just as they have been fully known.

It is clear that the mirror is the completed New Testament. Our question is, "What do we see in the mirror?" Whatever it is, we can see it as if face to face, and what we see reveals us fully.

"For if anyone is a hearer of the word and not a doer, he is like a man who looks at his natural face in a *mirror*; for once he has looked at himself and gone away, he has immediately forgotten what kind of person he was. But one who *looks intently at the perfect law*, the law of liberty, and abides by it, not having become a forgetful hearer but an effectual doer, this man shall be blessed in what he does" (James 1:23–25).

"I am the resurrection and the life; he who believes in Me shall live even if he dies."
JOHN 11:25

Again the *mirror* is used, this time in reference to the perfect law. There are two kinds of lookers—those who look, then turn and forget, and those who continue to look intently into the mirror and act on what they see.

The completed New Covenant is the same as the perfect law, as contrasted with the Old Covenant, which made nothing perfect. Our question is, "What do we see in the mirror of the perfect law?"

"But we all, with unveiled face beholding as in a *mirror* the glory of the Lord, are being transformed into the same image from glory to glory, just as from the Lord, the Spirit" (II Corinthians 3:18)!

We, if we have an unveiled face, see in the mirror of the New Testament [and perfect law] the *glory of the Lord*—the resurrected Christ!

The result of the intent look into the mirror, and abiding by what is seen, is that the effectual doer is transformed into the same image—that of the resurrected Christ. Note that from the very beginning—from our immersions into Christ—we were to view ourselves as already resurrected. If a person's picture, held intently in front of him, is that of the glory of the Lord, that is what he will become!

From our present state of glory—that of participating in the likeness of Jesus' resurrection—to our future state of glory when Jesus comes again, the transformation process will be occurring. And at the last trumpet, when this mortal puts on immortality, then we shall be like Him. The body of this humble state will be changed into conformity with the body of His glory! We are being transformed into the image of the glory of the Lord, from present glory to future glory.

And note who is the driving force behind all this transformation—the Lord, the Spirit. This is why He—as the promise—is the central message of the New Testament, and as the mystery, the central message of the Old Testament. As the hope of glory within, He is the guarantee of our ultimate transformation to be like Christ.

Summary And Conclusion

In the beginning man lost his fellowship with God because of sin. That fellowship was never capable of full restoration until Jesus came to reconcile us to the Father. Man as a spiritual being has deep inner needs which can only be met in fellowship with the Father. It is through the promised Holy Spirit that our fellowship is restored: "If anyone loves Me," Jesus said, "he will keep My word; and My Father will love him, and *We will come to him, and make our abode with him*" (John 14:23).

It is by working within, with our spirits, that the Holy Spirit, Christ in you, the hope of glory, makes us to be like Christ. For "though our outer man is decaying, yet our inner man is being renewed day by day" (II Corinthians 4:16). It is this renewing action that continues to save us—the washing of regeneration wiped out past sins, the renewing of the Spirit takes care of our present: "He saved us, not on the basis of deeds which we have done in righteousness, but according to His mercy, by the washing of regeneration and *renewing by the Holy Spirit*, whom He poured out on us richly through

Jesus Christ our Savior" (Titus 3:5).

God's purpose, then, is to conform us to the image of the resurrected Christ. To arrive at that conclusion, we examined the following "cipher" words:

promise

mystery

glory

mirror

In "deciphering" the passages of Scripture where these words were found, we reached the following conclusions:

1. Forgiveness of sins is not the central message of the New Testament. It is the vehicle to the promise of the indwelling Holy Spirit.

2. The message of the Old Testament is not simply Christ—but the mystery of Christ in you.

3. Glory is primarily a description of Jesus in His resurrected state.

4. In the mirror of the completed New Testament and perfect law we see the image of the resurrected Christ, and by looking intently into that image are transformed into the same image.

IV. WHAT DOES THE SPIRIT DO FOR THE CHRISTIAN?

He Enables Us To Be Like Christ

Jesus, when He walked in the flesh, consisted of body, soul, and spirit, just as we do. His body hung on the cross, His soul descended to Hades, and to His Father He commended His Spirit. Who is the Spirit of Jesus? The Holy Spirit, or the Spirit of Christ (see Acts 16:7).

Note, then, that the Spirit who has come to live in our bodies and make them His temple lived in flesh once before. And in that body, He proved what He can do. "For God has not given us a spirit of timidity, but of power and love and discipline" (II Timothy 1:7). The same Spirit of power—of dynamic determination—that once set His face resolutely to go to Jerusalem, that drove the men, sheep, oxen, and doves out of the temple—now lives in us. The same Spirit of love who said, "Father, forgive them, for they don't know what they're doing" now lives in us. The same Spirit of discipline—who not for the smallest fraction of a second ever let His flesh control His actions—now lives in us. Is He somehow less capable in our bodies than He was in His own, or is the problem with us?

"For you have not received a spirit of slavery leading to fear again, but you have received a spirit of adoption as sons by which we cry out, 'Abba! Father!'" (Romans 8:15). Fear no longer has any grip on us. As God's sons, we are free to press on to perfection.

He Helps Us Crucify The Flesh

"For the flesh sets its desire against the Spirit, and the Spirit against the flesh; for these are in opposition to one another, so that you may not do the things that you please" (Galatians 5:17). It is clear that we have a war going on within us. The opposing armies are the forces of the flesh (the body) against the forces of the spirit. If the flesh wins, we will experience eternal death; if the spirit wins, we will experience eternal life (Romans 8:5–8).

In such a war, it is important that we have little tests by which we may look within ourselves to see how the battle is going.

First Paul lists the works of the flesh: "Now the deeds of the flesh are evident, which are: immorality, impurity, sensuality, idolatry, sorcery, enmities, strife, jealousy, outbursts of anger, disputes, dissensions, factions, envying, drunkenness, carousing, and things like these" (Galatians 5:19–21). He then points out "that those who practice such things shall not inherit the kingdom of God." It is important to note that the Holy Spirit uses the word *practice*. We may stumble and exhibit the works of the flesh on occasion, but when such deeds become our practice, it is a definite warning that the flesh is winning the war; and only strong measures of repentance from a sincere heart will turn the tide.

In contrast, Paul lists the "fruit of the Spirit" (Galatians 5:22,23). Such fruit consists of "love, joy, peace, patience, kindness, goodness, faithfulness, gentleness, self–control."

It is important to note a common quality of all such fruit. Love, for example, is commanded by the Lord Jesus Christ. "This I command you, that you love one another" (John 15:17). Christian love is a quality which we achieve by mental effort, and Jesus commanded us to make the mental effort. The same is true with joy (James 1:2) and the other fruit of the Spirit. Such qualities result from a transformed mind—those who live by the Spirit *will* walk by the Spirit.

It is also important to understand the word picture he uses—*fruit* of the Spirit. An apple tree blossoms in the spring; it does not bear fruit until fall. After a person is born again, it is some time before the blossoming new creature bears the fruit of the Spirit. We must understand this so that we don't get too impatient with ourselves. God's patience while we grow makes the New Covenant the "perfect law, the law of liberty" (James 1:25), with opportunities to make mistakes without our errors condemning us.

"Now those who belong to Christ Jesus have crucified the flesh with its passions and desires" (Galatians 5:24). By helping us to bear such fruit, the Spirit helps us to crucify the flesh with its passions. Without His help, we couldn't begin to accomplish that great task.

The Spirit Leads Us

"For all who are being led by the Spirit of God, these are the sons of God" (Romans 8:14).

1.   The primary manner in which the Spirit leads us is through the Bible. Jesus said, "It is the Spirit who gives life; the flesh profits nothing; *the words that I have spoken* to you are spirit and are life" (John 6:63). In another place He said, as a driving point in an argument with some recalcitrant Jews, "the Scripture cannot be broken" (John 10:35). God simply will not do anything contrary to what the Bible says. Hence, Paul writes, "All Scripture is inspired by God and profitable for teaching [doctrine], for reproof, for correction, for training in righteousness; that the man of God may be adequate, equipped for every good work" (II Timothy 3:16,17).

2.   The second way in which the Spirit leads us is through our con-

sciences. Paul told Timothy to keep "a good conscience" (II Timothy 1:19). Christians are warned, for example, about "wounding the conscience" (I Corinthians 8:12) of a weaker brother. The Scripture also speaks of those who are "seared in their own conscience as with a branding iron" (I Timothy 4:2). The conscience is a guide given by God and a Christian is to follow his and not weaken another's.

The conscience is not a totally reliable guide, however. The written word is clear, precise, and perfectly delineates between right and wrong. The conscience by comparison is unreliable, as Paul makes clear: "I am conscious of nothing against myself, yet I am not by this acquitted" (I Corinthians 4:4).

3. The Spirit leads through events over which we have no control. In Acts 16:7,8, Paul was trying to preach the gospel in certain areas of what is now Turkey. But in every case the Spirit prevented him, arranging instead for him to go to Macedonia. So today "God has placed the members, each one of them, in the body, just as He desired" (I Corinthians 12:18).

The Christian should be cautioned against relying too heavily upon (2) and (3). The Bible is written as God's means of communicating to us. God expects us to "be diligent" in studying His word, and in this way becoming imitators of Paul and especially the Lord Jesus. Jesus died on His own initiative (John 10:18), and God expects us to follow in His footsteps in acting on our own initiative also.

The Spirit Intercedes For Us

"And in the same way the Spirit also helps our weakness; for we do not know how to pray as we should, but the Spirit Himself intercedes for us with groanings too deep for words; and He who searches the hearts knows what the mind of the Spirit is, because He intercedes for the saints according to the will of God" (Romans 8:26,27).

One time my family and I had been to visit my parents some 50 miles away. It was late at night as we were coming back and a snow storm had just coated the highway with an inch of ice. As we came over a hill I could see the flashing lights of a snowplow down below. At first it looked to me like it was on my side of the road, so I touched by brakes—it was so icy it seemed like I gained speed. As we came closer, I could see that the plow was sitting cockeyed in the middle of the road. I knew I couldn't stop, so I tried to go to the right. As we went past, there wasn't quite enough room for the car and the right front wheel went off the edge of the road. I remember saying (I had rolled a car once before, and this felt like it was going to do the same), "I pray, Father, I pray!"

As I said those words the car hit a bump that turned us perpendicular to the road, and we took a "bobsled run" to the bottom of the hill. When we went out the next morning to look at the place where we went off the road, we could see—in the words of the officer who checked out the accident—that "it was a miracle you didn't roll."

I have no way of knowing for sure whether it was just coincidence or whether the Holy Spirit "interceded with groanings too deep to be uttered." But I believe this is a good example of the way He would apply this verse of Scripture if it were His choice.

Summary

We received the same Spirit in our bodies as lived in Jesus—the Spirit of power, love, and discipline. He helps us to crucify the flesh, He leads us that we might be the sons of God, and He intercedes for us in prayer.

V. EXHORTATIONS FROM THE SPIRIT
Be Filled With The Spirit

We have been given the command: "And do not get drunk with wine, for that is dissipation, but be filled with the Holy Spirit" (Ephesians 5:18). How are we to be filled with the Spirit? Paul gives us three things we can do to be filled with the Spirit of God.

1. "Speaking to one another in psalms and hymns and spiritual songs, singing and making melody with your heart to the Lord" (Ephesians 5:19).

Singing is a way of being filled with the Spirit! Before Jesus crossed

40

the brook to the Garden of Gethsemane, He and the apostles sang a hymn (Matthew 26:30). When Paul and Silas were locked in the jail house in the Macedonian city of Philippi, at midnight, in the inner prison "Paul and Silas were praying and singing hymns of praise to God" (Acts 16:25).

Paul and Silas had positive mental attitudes! Many others in the same situation—locked in the dungeon—would have been saying, "Why me, Lord?" But they were singing praises to God!

To be filled with the Spirit, we must speak to one another in psalms and hymns and *spiritual* songs. And the times when we least feel like singing are especially the times when we must sing!

God says—be filled with the Spirit. The exhortation comes—sing! The Dale Carnegie course (which specializes in helping people have a positive mental attitude) teaches its students this principle: Act enthusiastic and you'll be enthusiastic!

If we'll sing, we will be filled with the Holy Spirit.

The Holy Spirit wants us to sing psalms and hymns and spiritual songs. Only in this way can we be filled with the Spirit. If we insist on confusing our minds with rock–and–roll music, or with country–western music, we will never be able to be *filled* with the Spirit. It's not a law—it's a choice. Do we want to be like Jesus?

2. "Always giving thanks for all things in the name of our Lord Jesus Christ to God, even the Father" (Ephesians 5:20).

A second important practical way of being filled with the Spirit is to *always* give thanks for *all* things. Suppose that it's 20° below zero, the wind is blowing, and it's snowing outside. It's absolutely necessary that you be able to go downtown for some important appointment.

You go out to start the car. It won't start. Do you give thanks to God from the very depths of your heart, remembering that to be filled with the Spirit we give thanks for *all* things—always? Or do you say to yourself, "Why me, Lord?"

Remember Joseph—the lad with the coat of many colors? Joseph's brothers sold him into slavery in Egypt. He was doing well for his master when the master's wife got wrong ideas into her head. Joseph ended up in jail—innocent, just trying to do a good job.

While in jail, because of his spirit—his attitude—he was placed in charge of all the other prisoners. But when he interpreted the dreams of the king's butler and baker (telling the baker that would be hanged, but that the butler would be restored to the service of Pharaoh) things took a downturn. He asked the butler to remember him before the king. And the butler forgot him!

Was Joseph in the jail house saying, "Why me, Lord?" No, he wasn't! He was still trusting God, and God rewarded him by eventually placing him in charge of all Egypt.

We need to remember Romans 8:28: "And we know that God *causes* all things to work together for good to those who love God, to those who are called according to His purpose." And then we need to give thanks for all things!

3. "And be subject to one another in the fear of Christ" (Ephesians 5:21). What has being subject to another to do with being filled with the Spirit?

    On the night in which Jesus was betrayed, as they were eating the Lord's Supper together, "there also arose a dispute among them as to which of them was regarded to be the greatest" (Luke 22:24).

While this dispute was going on, Jesus girded Himself with a towel and was washing their feet. When He had finished, He explained to them: "I gave you an example that you also should do as I did to you" (John 13:15).

Jesus came to serve, not to be served (Matthew 20:28). And He had joy in so doing: "These things I have spoken to you, that My joy may be in you, and that your joy may be made full" (John 15:11).

There is great joy in serving voluntarily. We must serve—we must be subject to one another and be each other's slave—in order to be filled with the Spirit and to be like our serving Savior.

Do Not Grieve The Spirit

The Holy Spirit is our Helper, but He can be grieved. So He warns, "Do not grieve the Holy Spirit of God, by whom you were sealed for the day of redemption" (Ephesians 4:30).

If we grieve Him long enough, as an unwanted guest in our lives, He will leave; or at least no longer seal us for the day of redemption. "For in the case of those who have once been enlightened and have tasted of the heavenly gift and have been made *partakers of the Holy Spirit*, and have tasted the good word of God and the powers of the age to come, and then have fallen away, it is impossible to renew them again to repentance . . ." (Hebrews 6:4–6). There are those who have once been partakers of the Holy Spirit, but He is so grieved that it is now impossible to renew them to repentance.

Perhaps the song children sing in Bible school expresses it best:

> *"Be careful little eyes what you see.*
> *Be careful little eyes what you see.*
> *For the Father up above is looking down in love,*
> *So be careful little eyes what you see."*

The same holds true for the ears, the hands and feet, the mouth, the mind. Do not grieve the Holy Spirit of God!

Do Not Quench The Holy Spirit

A fire is quenched when someone throws cold water on it to put it out. There are many people who are throwing cold water on the Holy Spirit's ideas. But He warns, "Do not quench the Spirit" (I Thessalonians 5:19).

There are people who claim that they can't pray in public because they are too shy. There are people who claim that they can't talk to others about Christ because they don't have the personality for it. There are women who claim they can't be in subjection to their husbands because they aren't made that way. Such people do not understand the *new creation*.

When we were buried with Christ in immersion, we buried our old personalities and natures. And we became new creatures with new personalities and new natures. And we can do whatever the Bible says we can do. Let's not quench the Spirit!

Making The Body Our Slave

In I Corinthians 9:24–27, Paul emphasized the importance of mental control over the body. "Do you not know that those who run in a race all run, but only one receives the prize. Run in such a way that you may win. And everyone who competes in the games exercises self–control in all things. They then do it to receive a perishable wreath, but we an imperishable. Therefore I run in such a way, as not without aim; I box in such a way, as not beating the air; *but I buffet my body and make it my slave*, lest possibly, after I have preached to others, I myself should be disqualified."

The body always wants to do the easy thing. It is our former nature to look for the easy job, to want more vacation time, more time to relax. The body wants to quit early today and to stay in bed a little longer tomorrow.

But we need to treat our bodies like children—they need buffeting occasionally. If we let our bodies get by without doing what they are supposed to today, they'll press for an easier time tomorrow.

Any runner knows that he must give it all he's got in order to win the race. The Holy Spirit tells us to so run!

Any athlete knows that he must be in rigorous training at all times to be in condition for the Olympics. The Holy Spirit tells us that the prize in the Spiritual Olympics is much more worth the rigorous training.

A football player must run the right direction to make his points count for the right team; a boxer knows he must make his punches count. The Christian must set goals for himself—he must run the right direction, and he must make his punches count.

The Holy Spirit will help us to make our bodies our slaves if we'll follow the directions given in the Bible. But it is going to take the mental discipline and training that a coach requires of his team. And if we refuse to make our bodies our slaves, even though we may have preached to many others, we will be disqualified. Let's go, team!

Summary

The Holy Spirit exhorts us to be filled with the Spirit, telling us how to do so:

1. Singing and making melody in our hearts to the Lord.
2. Always giving thanks for all things.
3. Being subject to one another in the fear of Christ.

The Spirit warns us not to grieve Him, not to quench Him, and to make our bodies our slaves.

All these exhortations from the Spirit involve mental discipline. The Holy Spirit does not miraculously change us so that we are instantly like Christ. He lets us have the joy of making ourselves be like Him, with His coaching help.

VI. LIFE! IN JESUS

"In Him was *life*, and the *life* was the light of men" (John 1:4). John also records that Jesus said, "I am the way, and the truth, and the *life*; no one comes to the Father, but through Me" (John 14:6).

Life is in Jesus Christ. But we sometimes have a difficult time understanding what *life* is.

One of the most important verses of Scripture is Romans 8:2, "For the law of the Spirit of life in Christ Jesus has set you free from the law of sin and death." What is the law of the Spirit of life, as contrasted with the law of sin and death?

A law states a cause and effect relationship—in the physical realm, expressed usually in mathematical form. The law of sin and death (codified by the Ten Commandments) is a very clear cause and effect relationship—You sin, therefore you die. Its important corollary is that if you do not sin, you will live.

The law of sin and death, however, is the ministry of death (II Corinthians 3:7). By continually forcing the individual's attention back into the stone tablets, the inner picture which develops is that of being a sinner. And if the individual continues to view himself as a sinner, that is precisely how he will act. The focus of our thoughts is to be turned from the "push" of "what not to be" to the "pull" of "what to be."

This is the law of the Spirit of life in Christ Jesus. In being born again we now have the potential of being like Christ! We are pressing on, following "the upward call of God in Christ Jesus" (Philippians 3:14). We have a new attitude—we *want* to be like Christ! We don't have to worship God—we want to! We don't have to go to church—we want to!

Many Christians have never seen the vision of enthusiasm of wanting to do things for God. They are still laboring under the law of sin and death. So they think they *have to* go to church. They think they *have to* talk to others about Jesus. There are a lot of things they think they *have to* do, and Christianity is a real burden to them. Their problem—their attitudes!

To this point the apostle John writes: "For this is the love of God, that we keep His commandments; and His commandments are not burdensome" (I John 5:3). His commandments are not burdensome—if they are becoming burdensome, we need to look deeper for help! "For whatever is born of God *overcomes* the world; and this is the victory that has overcome the world—our faith" (I John 5:4).

Our faith has overcome the world. For us there is no situation too hopeless, no problem too complex, no mountain too big to move. For us it is simply a matter of developing our faith, increasing our belief level joyfully to understand that God "is able to do exceedingly abundantly beyond all that we ask or think, according to the *power* that works within us" (Ephesians 3:20).

With the power of the Spirit within, we can turn this world upside down as we one by one strive mightily to present every man perfect in Christ. We can give desperately needed life to the dying world around us. "He who believes in Me," Jesus said, "from His innermost being shall flow rivers of living water" (John 7:37,38). We have seen that He was speaking of the Spirit, whom we have received. Let's let those rivers flow!

Summary

There is joy in living in Christ because we know that God will do great things through us when we commit ourselves to keeping His commandments. God can do more than we can even ask or think through the Holy Spirit who lives in us.

CONCLUSION

The basic conclusions reached in this study are as follows:

1. It is possible for the Christian, because he is a new creation following his immersion into Christ, to become like Christ.

2. This new creation must be developed in a continual process of renewing the mind—by seeing the picture of the resurrected Christ, developing the picture of the resurrected Christ, and keeping focused on the picture of the resurrected Christ.

3. God's purpose through the ages was to send the Holy Spirit to those who are faithful to Him, so that fellowship with God may be restored, and the faithful may become perfect like their heavenly Father. God communicates this exciting concept, in words such as *promise, mystery, glory,* and *mirror,* that we might better understand His purpose. Forgiveness of sin is a vehicle to the indwelling Spirit, and as a key concept of God, must be understood in comprehending the message of the New Testament. The message of the Old Testament is not merely Christ, but Christ in you. In the mirror of the perfect revelation of God—the completed New Testament and perfect law—we see the image of the glory of the resurrected Christ, and in consequence are being transformed into that same image.

4. The Holy Spirit leads him that he might be a son of God, and intercedes for the Christian in prayer.

5. Christians are exhorted to be filled with God's Spirit, not to grieve the Spirit, nor quench Him, and to make our bodies our slaves.

6. Life in Jesus is freedom from the old way of thinking. The Christian joyfully does what God wants in a concentrated effort to be like Christ. He believes that God is able to do exceedingly abundantly beyond what he asks or thinks, by the power of the Holy Spirit who works within.

THE NEW CREATION

Instructions: *This set of questions is divided into two sections: <u>Specific Questions</u> and <u>General Questions.</u> The Specific Questions bring out many details in the study, and help you to understand many of the important points, and where to find answers to many common questions in the scripture. The General Questions help you to pick out the major ideas and concepts in the study. You may use your Bible and study booklet for the Specific Questions, but try to answer the General Questions from memory.*

Each section is divided into subsections, each of which has its own type of questions and its attendant instructions.

Specific Questions

True or False?

_____ 1. The good news of Christianity is not centered on forgiveness of sins.

_____ 2. Jesus said, "You must be born again."

_____ 3. Forgiveness of sins is obtained through asking Jesus into your heart.

_____ 4. In order to live a new life in Christ, the Christian finds that he needs help.

_____ 5. The apostle Paul stated, "Neither is circumcision anything, nor uncircumcision, but a new creation."

_____ 6. Unless we understand what God envisions us as being, Christianity is nothing more than an extremely burdensome set of rules which are grudgingly obeyed.

Multiple choice. More than one answer may be correct; show all correct answers.

_____ 1. If any man is in Christ:

   a) He is a new creature.

   b) He got there by being immersed into Christ.

   c) He is entitled to walk on water.

   d) Old things have passed away, new things have come.

_____ 2. Being born again:

   a) Is the result of entering into your mother's womb again.

   b) Is the result of being born of both water and Spirit.

   c) Occurs as described in Acts 2:38.

   d) Never happens any more.

_____ 3. We are commanded in the New Testament:

   a) To sleep all day.

   b) To follow in the footsteps of Jesus.

   c) To be conformed to the image of Christ.

   d) To be an imitator of Jesus Christ.

_____ 4. Jesus commanded:

   a) Beware of the dogs.

   b) You must be born again.

   c) Close the closet door when you pray.

   d) Therefore you are to be perfect as your heavenly Father is perfect.

_____ 5. John the Immerser:

   a) Is a part of the kingdom of God.

   b) Never entered the kingdom of God on earth.

   c) Was greater than all the Old Testament greats.

   d) Is overshadowed by even the least in the kingdom of God.

_____ 6. The kingdom of heaven:

   a) Is the church.

   b) Is the body of Christ.

   c) Consists of all those who have been born again.

   d) Is yet to come.

_____ 7. The new potential:
   a) Consists of a new high voltage regulator.
   b) Is the result of being born again.
   c) Consists of all those who have been born again.
   d) Opens the doorway for a new self image.

_____ 8. The new creature:
   a) Has a new potential.
   b) Is born, not of man, but of God.
   c) Needs to sleep more.
   d) Spends a lot of time going over past mistakes.

_____ 9. In Romans 6:1-11:
   a) It is clear that we are buried with Christ in immersion.
   b) The old man is crucified.
   c) A person is raised to walk in newness of life.
   d) Is now to think of himself as being dead to sin but alive to God in Christ Jesus.

_____ 10. In Jesus' resurrection:
   a) Jesus is now an angel.
   b) Is described as dead to sin but alive to God.
   c) The devil could tempt Him no more.
   d) A Christian through immersion has participated in the resurrection of Christ and is now to think of himself as Jesus was when He was resurrected.

_____ 11. The new self:
   a) Is to be put on after the old self is laid aside.
   b) Is being renewed in the true knowledge of the image of the one who created him.
   c) Has been created in the likeness of God in righteousness, holiness, and truth.
   d) Is that we can be like Christ.

Fill in the blanks.

1. Christianity is some place between your _____ and the _____ _____ _____ _____.

2. The Bible says that we must believe with our _____ that God raised _____ from the _____; but that is not separate and distinct from _____ _____.

3. Come now, let us _____ together, says the _____.

4. We must _____ that we have the _____ of being exactly like Christ.

5. If we do not believe that we can be _____ _____, it is certain that we _____.

6. For what the _____ could not do, _____ as it was through the _____, God did, sending _____ _____ _____ in the likeness of _____ _____ and as an _____ _____ _____, He condemned sin in the _____ in order that the _____ of the Law might fulfilled in _____ who do not walk according to the _____ but according to the _____.

7. Law could never _____ the kind of _____ who could keep it.

8. In sending Jesus as an _____ for sin, the past is _____ _____. Yesterday was _____ to the cross with _____, and our excuse that we cannot be _____ today because we were not perfect _____ was nailed there with our sins.

52

9. In coming in the likeness of sinful _____, Jesus demonstrated that it was possible for the _____ _____ to control the outer man so that is does not _____. Jesus proved to us that it _____ _____ _____.

10. I can _____ _____ _____ through _____ who _____ me.

Answer the following questions.

1. What is the difference between life and death? _____

   _____

   _____ _____

   _____ _____

   _____

2. Once we realize that we can be like Jesus and believe that we have that potential, what is our next step? _____

   _____

   _____

   _____

3. What does it mean to set our minds? _____

   _____

   _____

   _____

   _____

   _____

   _____

4. What does it mean to set our minds on the things of the flesh? __

_____

_____

_____

_____

_____

5. List four things of the Spirit that a Christian must set his mind on: _____

_____

_____

_____

_____

6. What does it mean to set our minds on the things of the kingdom of God?_____

_____

_____

_____

_____

_____

7. What are four things we must set our minds on in order to seek and save the lost? _____

_____

_____

_____

_____

8. What does it mean to work out our salvation with fear and trembling?

_____

_____

_____

_____

9. What does it mean to set the mind on things above? _____

_____

_____

_____

_____

True or False?

_____ 1. Once a Christian has set his mind to be like Christ, he faces another problem—he tends to lose his resolve.

_____ 2. A Christian is told not to worry about loss of resolve.

_____ 3. We are to be changed by the renewing of our minds.

_____ 4. Christians are to let their minds dwell on the things that are good and lovely.

_____ 5. Everything in Christianity is designed primarily to help us keep our minds set on being like Christ.

_____ 6. The Lord's Supper is not done in remembrance of Jesus—it is a ceremony done just for fun.

_____ 7. The early church met on the first day of the week to break bread in remembrance of Jesus.

_____ 8. God designed the assembly of the saints to help the Christian keep his mind focused on being like Christ.

_____ 9. Christians are to stimulate one another to be lazy and generally selfish.

_____ 10. God placed the members—each of them—in the body just as He desired.

_____ 11. Working with the local church should be a drudgery and an obligation.

_____ 12. Prayer is designed to focus our attention on being new creatures.

_____ 13. One of the elements of prayer designed to help us refocus our minds is that they are offered in Jesus' name.

_____ 14. God works with our attitudes in prayer in telling us to believe that we are going to receive what we pray for.

_____ 15. A person can pray with wrong motives and still have an acceptable set mind.

_____ 16. God uses prayer to develop persistence within us. We are to pray at all times and not lose heart.

_____ 17. An important way of getting the word of God inside our minds is to memorize the Bible.

_____ 18. The word of God does perform its work in those of us who believe.

_____ 19. Jesus said, "If you abide in Me and I abide in you, ask whatever you wish and it will be done for you" (John 15:7).

_____ 20. Man can live by bread alone.

_____ 21. Singing psalms and hymns and spiritual songs helps us to keep our minds focused on Jesus Christ.

_____ 22. If a Christian is really working at developing his new mind, then it is still acceptable for him to have worldly songs in his mind also.

_____ 23. One of the best ways to learn a subject well is to teach and explain it to others.

_____ 24. One of the most effective ways of developing the new creation is to become a teacher of God's word.

_____ 25. Teachers must be careful when they teach because they know that they shall incur a stricter judgment.

_____ 26. A person can make a half-hearted attempt at being like Jesus and still be acceptable to God.

Matching.

_____ 1. Man consists of body, soul, and spirit.   a) John 14:23

_____ 2. God made man in His image.

_____ 3. The promise is the Holy Spirit.   b) Galatians 3:13,14

_____ 4. The Old Testament men did not receive the Holy Spirit and apart from us could not be made perfect.   c) I Thessalonians 5:23

d) Genesis 1:26

_____ 5. Father and Son live inside the Christian through means of the Holy Spirit.   e) Hebrews 11:39,40

_____ 6. God saves us by two means: the washing of regeneration and renewing by the Holy Spirit.   f) Titus 3:5,6

Multiple choice. Show all correct answers; more than one answer may be correct.

_____ 1. The promise
  a) Is a general reference to the indwelling Holy Spirit.
  b) Is a "gopher" word.
  c) Is the reason that all men are shut up under sin.
  d) Is the reason that Christ redeemed us from the curse of the Law.

_____ 2. The Holy Spirit:
  a) Is called the Holy Spirit of promise in Ephesians 1:13.
  b) Is the purpose for which forgiveness of sins is the vehicle.
  c) Is a tag-end gift who simply comes as part of the most important New Testament message—forgiveness of sins.
  d) Is the promise of Acts 2:38,39.

3. All the great men of the Old Testament:
   a) Went to hell.
   b) Included John the Immerser.
   c) Did not receive the promise.
   d) Are exceeded by those who have received the promised Holy Spirit.

4. The mystery:
   a) Is another "cipher" word.
   b) Is Christ in you, which is another name for the Holy Spirit.
   c) Was hidden in the Old Testament.
   d) Is what must be preached in order to fully carry out the preaching of the word of God.

5. The blessing of Abraham:
   a) Was given by Abraham to his sons Jacob and Esau.
   b) Was a piece of the mystery hidden in Genesis 12:3.
   c) Is defined as the promise of the Spirit by Paul in Galatians 3:14.
   d) Makes it clear that the message of the Old Testament is not simply Christ, but "Christ in you."

6. Paul says:
   a) That the mystery was hidden from the past ages and generations.
   b) The mystery was that the Gentiles were fellow heirs, fellow members of the body, and fellow partakers of the promise.
   c) His purpose was to bring to light the administration of the mystery.
   d) That early Christians were to pray for him, that he might speak forth boldly and clearly the mystery of Christ.

7. Glory:
   a) Is a description of the resurrected state.
   b) Results from being glorified.
   c) Is an expression of praise derived from the exalted resurrected state.
   d) Is a prophecy of the American flag.

8. Isaiah:
   a) Wrote from his own imagination.
   b) Actually saw men from outer space and described it the best he could.
   c) Saw Yahweh of hosts in glory.
   d) Saw the resurrected Christ, according to John the apostle.

9. When Jesus comes again:
   a) Our bodies will be transformed into conformity with the body of His glory.
   b) We will have salvation or redemption of the body.
   c) We are guaranteed to be resurrected because of the indwelling Holy Spirit.
   d) Then will come about the kingdom of God on earth for which we eagerly await.

10. The mirror:
    a) Is the completed New Testament, the perfect law.
    b) Reveals the resurrected Christ.
    c) When we take an intent look into it, causes us to be transformed into the image of the resurrected Christ.
    d) Really does show who is the fairest of them all.

11. We are saved:
    a) By accepting Jesus into our hearts.
    b) By the washing of regeneration and renewing by the Holy Spirit.
    c) Even though our outer man is decaying, our inner man is being renewed day by day.
    d) By the Father and Son living within through the indwelling Spirit of God.

Answer the following questions.

1. Describe the Spirit we received, according to II Timothy 1:7 and Romans 8:16. Relate your answer to the person of Christ. _____

   _____

   _____

   _____

   _____

   _____

2. List the works of the flesh in Galatians 5:19-21. _____

   _____

   _____

   _____

   _____

3. List the fruit of the Spirit in Galatians 5:22,23. _____

   _____

   _____

   _____

   _____

4. Describe how the New Covenant is the perfect law, the law of liberty. _____

   _____

   _____

   _____

   _____

5. List three ways in which the Spirit of God leads the Christian. __

   _____

_____

_____

_____

6. Describe how the Spirit helps us to pray. _____

_____

_____

_____

_____

7. List three ways of being filled with the Spirit. _____

_____

_____

_____

_____

8. Describe what it means to grieve the Spirit. _____

_____

_____

_____

_____

9. Describe what it means to quench the Holy Spirit. _____

_____

_____

_____

_____

10. Describe the relationship expressed in I Corinthians 9:24-27 in regard to the body vs. the Spirit. _____

_____

_____

_____

_____

True or False?

_____ 1. In Jesus is life, and that life is the light of men.

_____ 2. Jesus said, "I am the way, the truth, and the life; no one comes to the Father but through Me."

_____ 3. The law of the Spirit of life in Christ Jesus is much like the law of sin and death.

_____ 4. If you live under the law of the Spirit of life in Christ Jesus, you want to do the things you do rather than feeling like you have to. There is a big difference.

_____ 5. The scripture speaks of Paul as following the upward call of God.

_____ 6. God's commandments are burdensome.

_____ 7. God is able to do exceedingly abundantly beyond all that we ask or think, according to the power of the Holy Spirit who works within.

_____ 8. The rivers of living water is another name for the Holy Spirit.

_____ 9. The abundant life consists of setting our minds to be like Jesus, and then doing the work necessary to renew our minds to be like Him.

General Questions

True or False?

_____   1.   For neither circumcision is anything nor uncircumcision, but a new creation.

_____   2.   The new creation concept is the most important concept there is in Christianity.

_____   3.   For the Christian all things are new.

_____   4.   The new creation begins when a person accepts Jesus into his heart.

_____   5.   John the Immerser was the greatest person ever born of human parents.

_____   6.   A Christian has a new potential because he is born of God.

_____   7.   The least Christian is never really going to be equal to John the Immerser.

_____   8.   The Christian is to be perfect just as his heavenly Father is perfect.

_____   9.   The most important teaching about immersion is that we are buried with Christ in immersion.

_____   10.   Immersion is the portrayal of the death, burial, and resurrection of Jesus Christ in which a person shares when he is born again.

_____   11.   When a person arises from the watery grave of Christian immersion, he is to think of himself as Jesus was when Jesus was resurrected.

Fill in the blanks.

1.   We must _____ that we can be like Christ.

2.   God said, "Come now, let us _____ together." The appeal that God makes to us is on the basis of our _____.

3.   The Bible says, "Faith comes from _____ and hearing by the _____ _____ _____."

4. What the Law could not do, _____ as it was through the _____, God did, sending His own son in the _____ _____ _____ _____ and as an _____ _____ _____. He condemned sin in the flesh, in order that the requirement of the _____ might be fulfilled in _____ who do not walk according to the flesh, but according to the _____.

5. _____ can do _____ things through Him who _____ _____ me.

6. The first element in _____ the new creature is to_____ that we can be like Christ.

7. We must _____ our minds.

8. The _____ set on the flesh is _____ but the mind set on the _____ is life and peace.

9. List four things that a Christian must set his mind on that would be regarded as things of the Spirit:

   _____

   _____

   _____

   _____

   _____

10. In order to become a new creature, a Christian must _____ focusing the_____ on God's things.

11. The scriptures say, "Be _____ by the renewing of the _____."

12. List five things that the Christian is to let his mind dwell on:

_____

_____

_____

_____

_____

_____

13. God has designed the church to help the _____ keep _____ _____ _____ on God's things.

14. List six things that was designed for the Christian to help him keep focusing his mind:

_____

_____

_____

_____

_____

_____

_____

15. "He who does not _____ with Me _____." There are no _____ _____. The new creature is developed by a _____ _____ of _____ the mind.

16. The individual's _____ must be _____ that he can be like _____, then he must be _____ to do so.

17. God helps the _____ to maintain his

_____ by providing the _____

_____ _____ _____.

Multiple Choice. More than one answer may be correct; show all correct answers.

_____ 1. The human being is:

    a) Body, soul, and spirit

    b) Lazy

    c) Different than animals

    d) Has spiritual needs which can be met only by fellowship with God

_____ 2. Man lost his fellowship with God:

    a) Because of poverty, ignorance, and disease

    b) Through the fall of Adam

    c) And his fellowship is restored only through Christ

    d) Forever

_____ 3. The promise of the Spirit:

    a) Is a side point of Christianity

    b) Is the central purpose of the New Testament

    c) Is so important that forgiveness of sins is only a means by which we might receive the promise

    d) Was a blessing which the Old Testament men possessed

_____ 4. The indwelling Spirit:

    a) Is both the mystery and the promise

    b) Transforms the Christian into the image of the resurrected Christ as he looks into the mirror of the New Testament

    c) Is the hope of glory

    d) Should never be discussed

_____ 5. The resurrection of the body:

    a) Is an illusory promise

    b) Is described as glory

    c) Is the awaited salvation or redemption

    d) Is the hope of glory

_____ 6. We have fellowship with God in Jesus:
   a) Because that fellowship was never lost
   b) Just as men throughout all times have had fellowship
   c) Through the Spirit who indwells us
   d) By all means

_____ 7. The inner man:
   a) Is hopeless
   b) Is regenerated in immersion
   c) Is continually being renewed by the Holy Spirit
   d) Opens the floodgates

True or False?

_____ 1. God's purpose throughout the ages has been to send the Holy Spirit to live in those who love and obey Him.

_____ 2. Fellowship with God through the Holy Spirit is given to Christians in the same way as Abraham enjoyed fellowship with God.

_____ 3. The Holy Spirit helps the Christian to crucify the flesh and bear the fruit of the Spirit.

_____ 4. The Spirit leads us primarily through speaking to our inner mind.

_____ 5. The Spirit leads Christians through the Bible, through their consciences, and through events over which they have no control.

_____ 6. The Holy Spirit can intercede for the Christian in prayer.

_____ 7. Christians are not commanded to be filled with the Spirit.

_____ 8. It is important that psalms and hymns and spiritual songs be a part of the Christian's mind in order for him to be filled with the Spirit.

_____ 9. A Christian only gives thanks for those things which he considers are for his benefit.

_____ 10. An important way of being filled with the Spirit is to be subject to one another in the fear of Christ.

_____ 11. Christians are exhorted not to grieve the Spirit.

_____ 12. If a Christian grieves the Spirit long enough, those who once had fellowship through the Spirit will be classified as those who were merely "once partakers."

_____ 13. Do not quench the Spirit.

_____ 14. A Christian's body is basically out of control, so there is no use in trying to bring it under control.

_____ 15. When we are filled with the Holy Spirit we lose control of our actions.

Matching.

_____ 1. In Him was life, and the life was the light of men.

a) Philippians 3:14

_____ 2. I am the way, and the truth, and the life; no one comes to the Father but through Me.

b) I John 5:3

_____ 3. God is able to do exceedingly abundantly beyond all that we ask or think, according to the power that works within us.

c) II Timothy 1:7

_____ 4. The law of the Spirit of life in Christ Jesus has set you free from the law of sin and death.

d) Ephesians 3:20

_____ 5. For this is the love of God, that we keep His commandments; and His commandments are not burdensome.

e) Romans 8:2

_____ 6. For God has not given us a spirit of timidity, but of power, love, and discipline.

f) John 1:4

_____ 7. I press on toward the goal for the prize of the upward call of God in Christ Jesus.

g) John 14:6

Made in the USA
Columbia, SC
13 January 2025

51724534R00046